THE NEW FOLGER LIBRARY
SHAKESPEARE

Designed to make Shakespeare's great plays available to all readers, the New Folger Library edition of Shakespeare's plays provides accurate texts in modern spelling and punctuation, as well as scene-by-scene action summaries, full explanatory notes, many pictures clarifying Shakespeare's language, and notes recording all significant departures from the early printed versions. Each play is prefaced by a brief introduction, by a guide to reading Shakespeare's language, and by accounts of his life and theater. Each play is followed by an annotated list of further readings and by a "Modern Perspective" written by an expert on that particular play.

Barbara A. Mowat is Director of Research at the Folger Shakespeare Library, Executive Editor of *Shakespeare Quarterly,* Chair of the Folger Institute, and author of *The Dramaturgy of Shakespeare's Romances* and of essays on Shakespeare's plays and their editing.

Paul Werstine is Professor of English at the Graduate School and at King's University College at the University of Western Ontario. He is general editor of the New Variorum Shakespeare and author of many papers and articles on the printing and editing of Shakespeare's plays.

Folger Shakespeare Library

The Folger Shakespeare Library in Washington, D.C., is a privately funded research library dedicated to Shakespeare and the civilization of early modern Europe. It was founded in 1932 by Henry Clay and Emily Jordan Folger, and incorporated as part of Amherst College in Amherst, Massachusetts, one of the nation's oldest liberal arts colleges, from which Henry Folger had graduated in 1879. In addition to its role as the world's preeminent Shakespeare collection and its emergence as a leading center for Renaissance studies, the Folger Shakespeare Library offers a wide array of cultural and educational programs and services for the general public.

FOLGER SHAKESPEARE LIBRARY

The Tragedy of

Macbeth

By

WILLIAM SHAKESPEARE

EDITED BY BARBARA A. MOWAT
AND PAUL WERSTINE

Simon & Schuster Paperbacks
NEW YORK LONDON TORONTO SYDNEY

Simon & Schuster Paperbacks
A Division of Simon & Schuster, Inc.
1230 Avenue of the Americas
New York, NY 10020

This Simon & Schuster New Folger trade paperback edition
September 2009

SIMON & SCHUSTER PAPERBACKS and colophon are registered
trademarks of Simon & Schuster, Inc.

For information regarding special discounts for bulk purchases,
please contact Simon & Schuster Special Sales at
1-866-506-1949 or business@simonandschuster.com.

The Simon & Schuster Speakers Bureau can bring authors to
your live event. For more information or to book an event,
contact the Simon & Schuster Speakers Bureau at
1-866-248-3049 or visit our website at www.simonspeakers.com.

Cover photo of Ian Merrill Peakes as Macbeth by Carol Pratt

Manufactured in the United States of America

10 9 8 7 6 5 4 3 2 1

ISBN 978-1-4391-7225-4

Contents

A Scottish king and his court.
From Raphael Holinshed, *The historie of Scotland* (1577).

Directors' Foreword

Blood runs down every page of *Macbeth*. Androgynous ghouls goad a war hero and his ambitious wife into becoming psycho-killers overnight. A ghostly, floating dagger drips blood. A king assassinates his own best friend, who rises from the dead, stalks the king, and drives him mad. A disembodied head and a monstrous talking baby rise from a bubbling witches' cauldron.

If you didn't know Shakespeare had written it, you'd instantly pigeonhole *Macbeth* as a supernatural horror thriller. Reviewers would say *Macbeth* leaves *A Nightmare on Elm Street, Friday the Thirteenth,* and *Psycho* in the dust—because *Macbeth* is not just a collection of heart-pounding moments of chills and terror. *Macbeth* burns itself into your heart with searing poetry, grisly humor, and deep psychological and philosophical insights.

A supernatural horror thriller. That was the concept that guided our 2008 production of *Macbeth.* Everybody knows that the words of *Macbeth* are great. We decided to give the play's shock, humor, and amazement their due as well.

We depicted the hallucinations and supernatural events with stage magic tricks. Why? Because *Macbeth* is a story about a world where "nothing is but what is not." And stage magic expresses that uneasy world perfectly. Magic places you firmly in the blood-soaked shoes of Mr. and Mrs. Macbeth. It lets you feel the same shiver of horror that Macbeth feels when the "Weird Sisters" melt into the air. When Lady Macbeth has a hideous nightmare of blood, you not only hear but *see* her hallucination, so you know exactly what she's feeling as she slowly goes insane.

If you compare the Folger text to the DVD of our production, you will see that we made lots of changes. Our first goal was to make sure audiences understood every moment, every syllable, every character, and every relationship. Our second was to make the journey passionate, evocative, and wildly entertaining. Our third was to make it truly effective for a modern audience. So sometimes we'd change a word that we thought would confuse a modern listener (for example, we substituted *miser* for the Elizabethan *niggard*). We sometimes intercut between two scenes, just as one might do in a movie. We pirated lines from minor characters to establish the Macduff family more prominently early in the play. And we added a mean-spirited little prologue to set the tone (as well as to satirize the overly perky pre-show speeches one sees at nearly every regional theater in America).

You'll notice that not everything the Porter says in our production was written by Shakespeare. The Porter scene, as Shakespeare wrote it, is raucous comedy. If you read the original text with explanatory notes, you'll probably be able to figure out what the jokes are supposed to mean, but you probably won't laugh. That's the problem with 400-year-old comedy. Jokes have to connect immediately or they're just not funny. If you're puzzling over the Porter's mention of "French hose," you're not laughing, and laughing is what you need to be doing at that moment of the play—to relieve the tension of the Duncan murder scene. So we invited our Porter, Eric Hissom, to take Shakespeare's premise (a drunken security guard answering the front door and pretending he's the doorman of Hell), and riff on it. Watch how Eric interweaves Hell-themed knock-knock jokes with Shakespeare's lines in a sort of flowchart that changed from night to night as Eric responded to the audience.

But if *Macbeth* is supernatural horror, why are there jokes at all? Because horror and humor are best friends. One feeds the other. In a horror movie, when the monster jumps out, we scream—then we laugh. Sure, our Weird Sisters are scary and disgusting, but when they chant over a cauldron full of dog tongues, lizard legs, and human body parts, it's so gross and over-the-top that it's funny. When Macbeth commits the most brutal and suspenseful murder ever, then remarks, " 'Twas a rough night," Shakespeare *wants* you to laugh at the gallows-humor understatement. As the Macbeths, we cast Ian Merrill Peakes and Kate Eastwood Norris, two experts in Shakespearean drama *and* comedy. Our thinking ran this way: if Mr. and Mrs. Macbeth start the play as somber, gloomy losers, it's hard to care when they have a tragic fall. But Ian and Kate are heroic, athletic, funny, and engaging; we like them the moment they walk onstage, so their doom touches us.

We doubt Shakespeare is rolling over in his grave at our choices. He wrote the magic, horror, and humor into the play. We think he'd agree that a great play, like a fine suit, needs occasional tailoring to make it fit the audience of its day.

If you like our version, don't give us directors too much credit. This show is a collaboration of actors, artisans, armorers, designers, choreographers, musicians, magicians, scholars, fight masters, and friends— all enabled by the combined resources of the Two River Theater Company and the Folger Theatre. The first time you view the video, we suggest watching it *without* a script in hand, just as you'd listen to a symphony before analyzing the score. Then study the original text and see what you think of the "tailorings" we did.

Finally, please remember: this isn't a movie. It's the recording of a theater show, made on a single afternoon in Washington, D.C. It's raw and rough. It is simply not the same as seeing the production live in the

theater. So we need you to invest a little more imagination than a movie would ask for. Put yourself into a
seat in that theater and "piece out our imperfections
with your thoughts." Then maybe you, too, will begin
to taste the blood.

Teller
Aaron Posner

Editors' Preface

In recent years, ways of dealing with Shakespeare's texts and with the interpretation of his plays have been undergoing significant change. This edition, while retaining many of the features that have always made the Folger Shakespeare so attractive to the general reader, at the same time reflects these current ways of thinking about Shakespeare. For example, modern readers, actors, and teachers have become interested in the differences between, on the one hand, the early forms in which Shakespeare's plays were first published and, on the other hand, the forms in which editors through the centuries have presented them. In response to this interest, we have based our edition on what we consider the best early printed version of a particular play (explaining our rationale in a section called "An Introduction to This Text") and have marked our changes in the text—unobtrusively, we hope, but in such a way that the curious reader can be aware that a change has been made and can consult the "Textual Notes" to discover what appeared in the early printed version.

Current ways of looking at the plays are reflected in our brief introductions, in many of the commentary notes, in the annotated lists of "Further Reading," and especially in each play's "Modern Perspective," an essay written by an outstanding scholar who brings to the reader his or her fresh assessment of the play in the light of today's interests and concerns.

As in the Folger Library General Reader's Shakespeare, which this edition replaces, we include explanatory notes designed to help make Shakespeare's language clearer to a modern reader, and we place the notes on the page facing the text that they explain. We also follow the earlier edition in including illustrations—of objects, of clothing, of mythological figures—from books and manuscripts in the Folger Library collection. We provide fresh accounts of the life of Shakespeare, of the publishing of his plays, and of the theaters in which his plays were performed, as well as an introduction to the text itself. We also include a section called "Reading Shakespeare's Language," in which we try to help readers learn to "break the code" of Elizabethan poetic language.

For each section of each volume, we are indebted to a host of generous experts and fellow scholars. The "Reading Shakespeare's Language" sections, for example, could not have been written had not Arthur King, of Brigham Young University, and Randal Robinson, author of *Unlocking Shakespeare's Language*, led the way in untangling Shakespearean language puzzles and shared their insights and methodologies generously with us. "Shakespeare's Life" profited by the careful reading given it by S. Schoenbaum, "Shakespeare's Theater" was read and strengthened by Andrew Gurr and John Astington, and "The Publication of Shakespeare's Plays" is indebted to the comments of Peter W. M. Blayney. We, as editors, take sole responsibility for any errors in our editions.

Our greatest debt is to the Folger Shakespeare Library: to Werner Gundersheimer, Director of the Library from 1984 to 2002, who made possible our edition, and to Gail Kern Paster, Director of the Library since 2002, whose interest and support are unfailing (and whose scholarly expertise is an invaluable resource); to Deborah Curren-Aquino and Christina Certo, who provide extensive editorial and production support; to Jean Miller, the Library's former Curator of Art, who combs the Library archives for illustrations, and to Julie Ainsworth, Head of Photography, who carefully photographs them; to the members of the Folger's Research Division; and, finally, to the generously supportive staff of the Library's Reading Room.

Barbara A. Mowat and Paul Werstine

Shakespeare's *Macbeth*

In 1603, at about the middle of Shakespeare's career as a playwright, a new monarch ascended the throne of England. He was James VI of Scotland, who then also became James I of England. Immediately, Shakespeare's London was alive with an interest in things Scottish. Many Scots followed their king to London and attended the theaters there. Shakespeare's company, which became the King's Men under James's patronage, now sometimes staged their plays for the new monarch's entertainment, just as they had for Queen Elizabeth before him. It was probably within this context that Shakespeare turned to Raphael Holinshed's history of Scotland for material for a tragedy.

In Scottish history of the eleventh century, Shakespeare found a spectacle of violence—the slaughter of whole armies and of innocent families, the assassination of kings, the ambush of nobles by murderers, the brutal execution of rebels. He also came upon stories of witches and wizards providing advice to traitors. Such accounts could feed the new Scottish King James's belief in a connection between treason and witchcraft. James had already himself executed women as witches. Shakespeare's *Macbeth* supplied its audience with a sensational view of witches and supernatural apparitions and equally sensational accounts of bloody battles in which, for example, a rebel was "unseamed . . . from the nave [navel] to th' chops [jaws]."

It is possible, then, that in writing *Macbeth* Shakespeare was mainly intent upon appealing to the new interests in London brought about by James's kingship. What he created, though, is a play that has fascinated generations of readers and audiences that care little about Scottish history. In its depiction of a man who murders his king and kinsman in order to gain the crown, only to lose all that humans seem to need in order to be happy—sleep, nourishment, friends, love—*Macbeth* teases us with huge questions. Why do people do evil knowing that it is evil? Does Macbeth represent someone who murders because fate tempts him? Because his wife pushes him into it? Because he is overly ambitious? Having killed Duncan, why does Macbeth fall apart, unable to sleep, seeing ghosts, putting spies in everyone's home, killing his friends and innocent women and children? Why does the success of Macbeth and Lady Macbeth—prophesied by the witches, promising the couple power and riches and "peace to all their nights and days to come"—turn so quickly to ashes, destroying the Macbeths' relationship, their world, and, finally, both of them?

In earlier centuries, Macbeth's story was seen as a powerful study of a heroic individual who commits an evil act and pays an enormous price as his conscience—and the natural forces for good in the universe—destroy him. More recently, his story has been applied to nations that overreach themselves, his speeches of despair quoted to show that Shakespeare shared late-twentieth-century feelings of alienation. Today, as Professor Susan Snyder describes in her "Modern Perspective" on the play (found at the back of this book), the line between Macbeth's evil and the supposed good of those who oppose him is being blurred, new attitudes about witches and witchcraft are being expressed, new questions raised about the ways that maleness and femaleness are portrayed in the play. As with so many of Shakespeare's plays, *Macbeth* speaks to each generation with a new voice.

After you have read the play, we invite you to read "*Macbeth:* A Modern Perspective" by Professor Susan Snyder of Swarthmore College.

Reading Shakespeare's Language

For many people today, reading Shakespeare's language can be a problem—but it is a problem that can be solved. Those who have studied Latin (or even French or German or Spanish) and those who are used to reading poetry will have little difficulty understanding the language of Shakespeare's poetic drama. Others, however, need to develop the skills of untangling unusual sentence structures and of recognizing and understanding poetic compressions, omissions, and wordplay. And even those skilled in reading unusual sentence structures may have occasional trouble with Shakespeare's words. Four hundred years of "static"—caused by changes in language and in life—intervene between his speaking and our hearing. Most of his immense vocabulary is still in use, but a few of his words are not, and, worse, some of his words now have meanings quite different from those they had in the sixteenth and seventeenth centuries. In the theater, most of these difficulties are solved for us by actors who study the language and articulate it for us so that the essential meaning is heard—or, when combined with stage action, is at least *felt*. When reading on one's own, one must do what each actor does: go over the lines (often with a dictionary close at hand) until the puzzles are solved and the lines yield up their poetry and the characters speak in words and phrases that are, suddenly, rewarding and wonderfully memorable.

Shakespeare's Words

As you begin to read the opening scenes of a play by Shakespeare, you may notice occasional unfamiliar words. Some are unfamiliar simply because we no longer use them. In the opening scenes of *Macbeth,* for example, you will find the words *aroint thee* (begone), *runnion* (a slatternly woman), *coign* (corner), *anon* (right away), *alarum* (a call to arms), *sewer* (a servant who oversees the serving of food), and *hautboy* (a very loud wind instrument designed for outdoor ceremonials, the forerunner of the orchestral oboe). Words of this kind are explained in notes to the text and will become familiar the more of Shakespeare's plays you read.

Some words are strange not because of the "static" introduced by changes in language over the past centuries but because these are words that Shakespeare is using to build a dramatic world that has its own geography and history and story. *Macbeth,* for example, builds, in its opening scenes, a location, a past history, and a background mythology by references to "the Western Isles," to "valor's minion," to "Bellona's bridegroom," to "thanes," "Sinel," "Glamis," and "Cawdor," to "kerns and gallowglasses," to "the Weïrd Sisters," to "Norweyan ranks," to "Inverness" and "Saint Colme's Inch." These "local" references build the Scotland that Macbeth and Lady Macbeth inhabit and will become increasingly familiar to you as you get further into the play.

In *Macbeth,* as in all of Shakespeare's writing, the most problematic words are those that we still use but that we use with different meanings. In the second scene of *Macbeth* we find the words *composition* (meaning "terms of peace") and *present* (meaning "immediate"); in the third scene, *choppy* is used where we would use "chapped" or "wrinkled," *addition* where we would use "title"; in the seventh scene, *receipt* is used to mean "receptacle." Again, such words will be explained in the notes to this text, but they, too, will become familiar as you continue to read Shakespeare's language.

Shakespeare's Sentences

In an English sentence, meaning is quite dependent on the place given each word. "The dog bit the boy" and "The boy bit the dog" mean very different things, even though the individual words are the same. Because English places such importance on the positions of words in sentences, on the way words are arranged, unusual arrangements can puzzle a reader. Shakespeare frequently shifts his sentences away from "normal" English arrangements—often in order to create the rhythm he seeks, sometimes to use a line's poetic rhythm to emphasize a particular word, sometimes to give a character his or her own speech patterns or to allow the character to speak in a special way. Again, when we attend a good performance of the play, the actors will have worked out the sentence structures and will articulate the sentences so that the meaning is clear. In reading for yourself, do as the actor does. That is, when you are puzzled by a character's speech, check to see if the words are being presented in an unusual sequence.

Look first for the placement of subject and verb. Shakespeare often places the verb before the subject (e.g., instead of "He goes," we find "Goes he"). In the opening scenes of *Macbeth*, when Ross says (1.3.101–2) "As thick as tale / Came post with post," and when the witch says (1.3.24) "Shall he dwindle, peak, and pine," they are using constructions that place the subject and verb in unusual positions. Such inversions rarely cause much confusion. More problematic is Shakespeare's frequent placing of the object before the subject and verb (e.g., instead of "I hit him," we might find "Him I hit"). Banquo's statement to the Weïrd Sisters at 1.3.57–58, "My noble partner / You greet with present grace and great prediction," is an example of such an inversion. (The normal order would be "You greet my noble partner with present grace and great prediction.") Lady Macbeth opens her soliloquy in 1.5 with such an inverted structure: "Glamis thou art, and Cawdor" (an inversion that increases the emphasis on the names "Glamis" and "Cawdor"); she uses another such inverted structure in 1.7.73–74 when she says to Macbeth, "his two chamberlains / Will I with wine and wassail . . . convince" (where the "normal" structure would be "I will convince [i.e., overcome] his two chamberlains with wine and wassail").

In some plays Shakespeare makes systematic use of inversions (*Julius Caesar* is one such play). In *Macbeth*, he more often uses sentence structures that depend instead on the separation of words that would normally appear together. (Again, this is often done to create a particular rhythm or to stress a particular word.) Malcolm's "This is the sergeant / Who, like a good and hardy soldier, fought / 'Gainst my captivity" (1.2.4–6) separates the subject and verb ("who fought"); the Captain's "No sooner justice had, with valor armed, / Compelled these skipping kerns to trust their heels" (1.2.32–33) interrupts the two parts of the verb "had compelled" (at the same time that it inverts the subject and verb; the normal order would be "No sooner had justice compelled . . ."); a few lines later, the Captain's "the Norweyan lord, surveying vantage, / With furbished arms and new supplies of men, / Began a fresh assault" (1.2.34–36) separates the subject and verb ("lord began"). In order to create for yourself sentences that seem more like the English of everyday speech, you may wish to rearrange the words, putting together the word clusters and placing the remaining words in their more familiar order. You will usually find that the sentences will gain in clarity but will lose their rhythm or shift their emphases. You can then see for yourself why Shakespeare chose his unusual arrangement.

Locating and, if necessary, rearranging words that "belong together" is especially necessary in passages that separate subjects from verbs and verbs from objects by long delaying or expanding interruptions—a structure that is used frequently in *Macbeth*. For example, when the Captain, at 1.2.11–25, tells the story of Macbeth's fight against the rebel Macdonwald, he uses a series of such interrupted constructions:

> *The merciless Macdonwald*
> (Worthy to be a rebel, for to that
> The multiplying villainies of nature
> Do swarm upon him) from the Western Isles
> Of kerns and gallowglasses *is supplied;*
>
> . . .
>
>   But all's too weak;
> For *brave Macbeth* (well he deserves that name),
> Disdaining Fortune, with his brandished steel,
> Which smoked with bloody execution,
> Like valor's minion, *carved out his passage* . . .

Here the interruptions provide details that catch the audience up in the Captain's story. The separation of the basic sentence elements "the merciless Macdonwald is supplied" forces the audience to attend to supporting details (of why he is worthy to be a villain, of how he has been supplied with soldiers from the Western Isles) while waiting for the basic sentence elements to come together. A similar effect is created when "brave Macbeth carved out his passage" is interrupted by a clause commenting on the word "brave" ("well he deserves that name"), by a phrase that describes Macbeth's mood ("Disdaining Fortune"), and by two further phrases, one of them the complex "with his brandished steel / Which smoked with bloody execution," and one of them a simple description, "Like valor's minion."

Occasionally, rather than separating basic sentence elements, Shakespeare simply holds them back, delaying them until much subordinate material has already been given. Lady Macbeth uses this kind of delaying structure when she says, at 1.6.22–24, "For those of old, / And the late dignities heaped up to them, / We rest your hermits" (where a "normally" constructed English sentence would have begun with the basic sentence elements "We rest your hermits"); Macbeth, in his famous soliloquy at 1.7.1–28, uses a delayed construction when he says (lines 2–7), "If th' assassination / Could trammel up the consequence and catch / With his surcease success, that but this blow / Might be the be-all and the end-all here, / But here, upon this bank and shoal of time, / We'd jump the life to come" (where the basic sentence elements "We'd jump the life to come" are delayed to the end of the very long sentence).

Shakespeare's sentences are sometimes complicated not because of unusual structures or interruptions or delays but because he omits words and parts of words that English sentences normally require. (In conversation, we, too, often omit words. We say, "Heard from him yet?" and our hearer supplies the missing "Have you." Frequent reading of Shakespeare—and of other poets—trains us to supply such missing words.) In *Macbeth*, Shakespeare uses omissions to great dramatic effect. At 1.3.105–8, Angus says to Macbeth, "We are sent / To give thee from our royal master thanks, / [We are sent] Only to herald thee into his sight, / Not [to] pay thee" (the omitted words, shown in brackets, add clarity but slow the speech). At 1.4.48–49, Duncan's cryptic "From hence to Inverness / And bind us further to you" would read, if the missing words were supplied, "Let us go from hence to Inverness, and may this visit bind us further to you." Lady Macbeth's soliloquy, at 1.5.15–33, would read, with the omitted subjects and verbs in place, "Thou wouldst be great, / [Thou] Art not without ambition, but [thou art] without / The illness [that] should attend it." Later in the soliloquy, at 1.5.51–54, she again omits words in saying, "Stop up th' access and passage to remorse, / [So] That no compunctious visitings of nature / [Will] Shake my fell purpose, nor keep peace between / Th' effect and it," and again at 1.7.80–82, where she asks Macbeth, "What [can]not [you and I] put upon / His spongy officers, who shall bear the guilt / Of our great quell?" In reading *Macbeth* one should stay alert for omitted words, since Shakespeare so often uses this device to build compression and speed in the language of this play.

Shakespearean Wordplay

Shakespeare plays with language so often and so variously that books are written on the topic. Here we will mention only two kinds of wordplay, puns and metaphors. A pun is a play on words that sound the same but have different meanings. In many plays (*Romeo and Juliet* is a good example) Shakespeare uses puns frequently; in *Macbeth* they are rarely found (except in such serious "punning" as Macbeth's "If it were done when 'tis done . . ."). Perhaps the play's most famous (and the most shocking) pun is Lady Macbeth's "If he do bleed, / I'll gild the faces of the grooms withal, / For it must seem their guilt" (2.2.71–73), where she seems to be playing with the double meaning of guilt/gilt. Such wordplay is rare in *Macbeth*.

A metaphor is a play on words in which one object or idea is expressed as if it were something else, something with which it shares common features. For instance, when Lady Macbeth says (1.5.28–29) "Hie thee hither / That I may pour my spirits in thine ear," she is using metaphoric language: the words that she wants to say to Macbeth are compared to a liquid that can be poured in the ear. Her instruction to Macbeth (1.5.76–78), "Look like th' innocent flower, / But be the serpent under 't," uses metaphor to draw a picture of how Macbeth should look in order to hide his evil intentions. Metaphors are often used when the idea being conveyed is hard to express; through metaphor, the speaker is given language that helps to carry the idea or the feeling to his or her listener—and to the audience. Lady Macbeth uses metaphor to convey her contempt for Macbeth's cowardice (1.7.39–42): "Was the hope drunk / Wherein you dressed yourself? Hath it slept since? / And wakes it now, to look so green and pale / At what it did so freely?" And Macbeth expresses his own lack of valid motivation before the murder through a horseback-riding metaphor (1.7.25–27): "I have no spur / To prick the sides of my intent, but only / Vaulting ambition, which o'erleaps itself. . . ."

Macbeth's Language

Each of Shakespeare's plays has its own characteristic language. In *Macbeth*, one notices particularly the deliberate imprecision of some of the play's words. Macbeth's lines (1.7.1–2) "If it were done when 'tis done, then 'twere well / It were done quickly" not only play with the imprecise verb "done" but also refer to some unnamed "it." In the next sentence, we learn that "it" is "th' assassination" (a word that Shakespeare invents for this play, as he does so many other words)—but the imprecision is characteristic of *Macbeth*'s language. We hear it again in Lady Macbeth's "Wouldst thou have that / Which thou esteem'st the ornament of life / And live a coward in thine own esteem. . . ?" (1.7.45–47) where "that which thou esteem'st the ornament of life" is, perhaps, the crown—or, perhaps, the kingship. The sense is clear, but the language seems deliberately vague, deliberately flowery, as if designed to cover over the serpent under it. In reading *Macbeth*, one must sometimes be content to get the gist of the characters' language, since in such lines as "the powers above / Put on their instruments" (4.3.279–80) no precise "translation" exists.

Implied Stage Action

Finally, in reading Shakespeare's plays you should always remember that what you are reading is a performance script. The dialogue is written to be spoken by actors who, at the same time, are moving, gesturing, picking up objects, weeping, shaking their fists. Some stage action is described in what are called "stage directions"; some is suggested within the dialogue itself. Learn to be alert to such signals as you stage the play in your imagination. When, in the third scene of *Macbeth*, Banquo says (1.3.44–47), "You seem to understand me / By each at once her choppy finger laying / Upon her skinny lips," the stage action is obvious. Again, his words to Macbeth (1.3.54–55), "Good sir, why do you start and seem to fear / Things that do sound so fair?," indicate that the actor playing Macbeth gestures in a fairly obvious way. It is less easy later in the scene to imagine exactly what is to take place just before Banquo says (1.3.82–83), "The earth hath bubbles, as the water has, / And these are of them. Whither are they vanished?" The director and the actors (and the reader, in imagination) must decide just how the witches "melt . . . into the wind." Learning to read the language of stage action repays one many times over when one reaches a crucial scene like that of the banquet and its appearing and disappearing ghost (3.2) or that of the final duel in 5.8, in both of which scenes implied stage action vitally affects our response to the play.

It is immensely rewarding to work carefully with Shakespeare's language so that the words, the sentences, the wordplay, and the implied stage action all become clear—as readers for the past four centuries have discovered. It may be more pleasurable to attend a good performance of a play—though not everyone has thought so. But the joy of being able to stage one of Shakespeare's plays in one's imagination, to return to passages that continue to yield further meanings (or further questions) the more one reads them—these are pleasures that, for many, rival (or at least augment) those of the performed text, and certainly make it worth considerable effort to "break the code" of Elizabethan poetic drama and let free the remarkable language that makes up a Shakespeare text.

Shakespeare's Life

Surviving documents that give us glimpses into the life of William Shakespeare show us a playwright, poet, and actor who grew up in the market town of Stratford-upon-Avon, spent his professional life in London, and returned to Stratford a wealthy landowner. He was born in April 1564, died in April 1616, and is buried inside the chancel of Holy Trinity Church in Stratford.

We wish we could know more about the life of the

world's greatest dramatist. His plays and poems are testaments to his wide reading—especially to his knowledge of Virgil, Ovid, Plutarch, Holinshed's *Chronicles,* and the Bible—and to his mastery of the English language, but we can only speculate about his education. We know that the King's New School in Stratford-upon-Avon was considered excellent. The school was one of the English "grammar schools" established to educate young men, primarily in Latin grammar and literature. As in other schools of the time, students began their studies at the age of four or five in the attached "petty school," and there learned to read and write in English, studying primarily the catechism from the Book of Common Prayer. After two years in the petty school, students entered the lower form (grade) of the grammar school, where they began the serious study of Latin grammar and Latin texts that would occupy most of the remainder of their school days. (Several Latin texts that Shakespeare used repeatedly in writing his plays and poems were texts that schoolboys memorized and recited.) Latin comedies were introduced early in the lower form; in the upper form, which the boys entered at age ten or eleven, students wrote their own Latin orations and declamations, studied Latin historians and rhetoricians, and began the study of Greek using the Greek New Testament.

Since the records of the Stratford "grammar school" do not survive, we cannot prove that William Shakespeare attended the school; however, every indication (his father's position as an alderman and bailiff of Stratford, the playwright's own knowledge of the Latin classics, scenes in the plays that recall grammar-school experiences—for example, *The Merry Wives of Windsor,* 4.1) suggests that he did. We also lack generally accepted documentation about Shakespeare's life after his schooling ended and his professional life in London

began. His marriage in 1582 (at age eighteen) to Anne
Hathaway and the subsequent births of his daughter
Susanna (1583) and the twins Judith and Hamnet
(1585) are recorded, but how he supported himself and
where he lived are not known. Nor do we know when
and why he left Stratford for the London theatrical
world, nor how he rose to be the important figure in
that world that he had become by the early 1590s.

We do know that by 1592 he had achieved some
prominence in London as both an actor and a playwright. In that year was published a book by the playwright Robert Greene attacking an actor who had the
audacity to write blank-verse drama and who was "in
his own conceit [i.e., opinion] the only Shake-scene in
a country." Since Greene's attack includes a parody of a
line from one of Shakespeare's early plays, there is little doubt that it is Shakespeare to whom he refers, a
"Shake-scene" who had aroused Greene's fury by suc-
cessfully competing with university-educated dramatists
like Greene himself. It was in 1593 that Shakespeare
became a published poet. In that year he published
his long narrative poem *Venus and Adonis;* in 1594,
he followed it with *The Rape of Lucrece.* Both poems
were dedicated to the young earl of Southampton
(Henry Wriothesley), who may have become Shakespeare's patron.

It seems no coincidence that Shakespeare wrote these
narrative poems at a time when the theaters were closed
because of the plague, a contagious epidemic disease
that devastated the population of London. When the
theaters reopened in 1594, Shakespeare apparently
resumed his double career of actor and playwright and
began his long (and seemingly profitable) service as an
acting-company shareholder. Records for December of
1594 show him to be a leading member of the Lord
Chamberlain's Men. It was this company of actors, later

named the King's Men, for whom he would be a principal actor, dramatist, and shareholder for the rest of his career.

So far as we can tell, that career spanned about twenty years. In the 1590s, he wrote his plays on English history as well as several comedies and at least two tragedies (*Titus Andronicus* and *Romeo and Juliet*). These histories, comedies, and tragedies are the plays credited to him in 1598 in a work, *Palladis Tamia*, that in one chapter compares English writers with "Greek, Latin, and Italian Poets." There the author, Francis Meres, claims that Shakespeare is comparable to the Latin dramatists Seneca for tragedy and Plautus for comedy, and calls him "the most excellent in both kinds for the stage." He also names him "mellifluous and honey-tongued Shakespeare": "I say," writes Meres, "that the Muses would speak with Shakespeare's fine filed phrase, if they would speak English." Since Meres also mentions Shakespeare's "sugared sonnets among his private friends," it is assumed that many of Shakespeare's sonnets (not published until 1609) were also written in the 1590s.

In 1599, Shakespeare's company built a theater for themselves across the river from London, naming it the Globe. The plays that are considered by many to be Shakespeare's major tragedies (*Hamlet, Othello, King Lear,* and *Macbeth*) were written while the company was resident in this theater, as were such comedies as *Twelfth Night* and *Measure for Measure*. Many of Shakespeare's plays were performed at court (both for Queen Elizabeth I and, after her death in 1603, for King James I), some were presented at the Inns of Court (the residences of London's legal societies), and some were doubtless performed in other towns, at the universities, and at great houses when the King's Men went on tour; otherwise, his plays from 1599 to 1608 were, so far as we know, performed only at the Globe. Between 1608 and

1612, Shakespeare wrote several plays—among them *The Winter's Tale* and *The Tempest*—presumably for the company's new indoor Blackfriars theater, though the plays seem to have been performed also at the Globe and at court. Surviving documents describe a performance of *The Winter's Tale* in 1611 at the Globe, for example, and performances of *The Tempest* in 1611 and 1613 at the royal palace of Whitehall.

Shakespeare wrote very little after 1612, the year in which he probably wrote *King Henry VIII*. (It was at a performance of *Henry VIII* in 1613 that the Globe caught fire and burned to the ground.) Sometime between 1610 and 1613 he seems to have returned to live in Stratford-upon-Avon, where he owned a large house and considerable property, and where his wife and his two daughters and their husbands lived. (His son Hamnet had died in 1596.) During his professional years in London, Shakespeare had presumably derived income from the acting company's profits as well as from his own career as an actor, from the sale of his play manuscripts to the acting company, and, after 1599, from his shares as an owner of the Globe. It was presumably that income, carefully invested in land and other property, that made him the wealthy man that surviving documents show him to have become. It is also assumed that William Shakespeare's growing wealth and reputation played some part in inclining the crown, in 1596, to grant John Shakespeare, William's father, the coat of arms that he had so long sought. William Shakespeare died in Stratford on April 23, 1616 (according to the epitaph carved under his bust in Holy Trinity Church) and was buried on April 25. Seven years after his death, his collected plays were published as *Mr. William Shakespeares Comedies, Histories, & Tragedies* (the work now known as the First Folio).

The years in which Shakespeare wrote were among

the most exciting in English history. Intellectually, the discovery, translation, and printing of Greek and Roman classics were making available a set of works and worldviews that interacted complexly with Christian texts and beliefs. The result was a questioning, a vital intellectual ferment, that provided energy for the period's amazing dramatic and literary output and that fed directly into Shakespeare's plays. The Ghost in *Hamlet,* for example, is wonderfully complicated in part because he is a figure from Roman tragedy—the spirit of the dead returning to seek revenge—who at the same time inhabits a Christian hell (or purgatory); Hamlet's description of humankind reflects at one moment the Neoplatonic wonderment at mankind ("What a piece of work is a man!") and, at the next, the Christian disparagement of human sinners ("And yet, to me, what is this quintessence of dust?").

As intellectual horizons expanded, so also did geographical and cosmological horizons. New worlds—both North and South America—were explored, and in them were found human beings who lived and worshiped in ways radically different from those of Renaissance Europeans and Englishmen. The universe during these years also seemed to shift and expand. Copernicus had earlier theorized that the earth was not the center of the cosmos but revolved as a planet around the sun. Galileo's telescope, created in 1609, allowed scientists to see that Copernicus had been correct: the universe was not organized with the earth at the center, nor was it so nicely circumscribed as people had, until that time, thought. In terms of expanding horizons, the impact of these discoveries on people's beliefs—religious, scientific, and philosophical—cannot be overstated.

London, too, rapidly expanded and changed during the years (from the early 1590s to around 1610) that Shakespeare lived there. London—the center of England's government, its economy, its royal court, its overseas trade—was, during these years, becoming an exciting metropolis, drawing to it thousands of new citizens every year. Troubled by overcrowding, by poverty, by recurring epidemics of the plague, London was also a mecca for the wealthy and the aristocratic, and for those who sought advancement at court, or power in government or finance or trade. One hears in Shakespeare's plays the voices of London—the struggles for power, the fear of venereal disease, the language of buying and selling. One hears as well the voices of Stratford-upon-Avon—references to the nearby Forest of Arden, to sheep herding, to small-town gossip, to village fairs and markets. Part of the richness of Shakespeare's work is the influence felt there of the various worlds in which he lived: the world of metropolitan London, the world of small-town and rural England, the world of the theater, and the worlds of craftsmen and shepherds.

That Shakespeare inhabited such worlds we know from surviving London and Stratford documents, as well as from the evidence of the plays and poems themselves. From such records we can sketch the dramatist's life. We know from his works that he was a voracious reader. We know from legal and business documents that he was a multifaceted theater man who became a wealthy landowner. We know a bit about his family life and a fair amount about his legal and financial dealings. Most scholars today depend upon such evidence as they draw their picture of the world's greatest playwright. Such, however, has not always been the case. Until the late eighteenth century, the William Shakespeare who lived in most biographies was the creation of legend and tradition. This was the Shakespeare who was supposedly caught poaching deer at Charlecote, the estate of Sir Thomas Lucy close by

Stratford; this was the Shakespeare who fled from Sir Thomas's vengeance and made his way in London by taking care of horses outside a playhouse; this was the Shakespeare who reportedly could barely read, but whose natural gifts were extraordinary, whose father was a butcher who allowed his gifted son sometimes to help in the butcher shop, where William supposedly killed calves "in a high style," making a speech for the occasion. It was this legendary William Shakespeare whose Falstaff (in *1* and *2 Henry IV*) so pleased Queen Elizabeth that she demanded a play about Falstaff in love, and demanded that it be written in fourteen days (hence the existence of *The Merry Wives of Windsor*). It was this legendary Shakespeare who reached the top of his acting career in the roles of the Ghost in *Hamlet* and old Adam in *As You Like It*—and who died of a fever contracted by drinking too hard at "a merry meeting" with the poets Michael Drayton and Ben Jonson. This legendary Shakespeare is a rambunctious, undisciplined man, as attractively "wild" as his plays were seen by earlier generations to be. Unfortunately, there is no trace of evidence to support these wonderful stories.

Perhaps in response to the disreputable Shakespeare of legend—or perhaps in response to the fragmentary and, for some, all-too-ordinary Shakespeare documented by surviving records—some people since the mid-nineteenth century have argued that William Shakespeare could not have written the plays that bear his name. These persons have put forward some dozen names as more likely authors, among them Queen Elizabeth, Sir Francis Bacon, Edward de Vere (earl of Oxford), and Christopher Marlowe. Such attempts to find what for these people is a more believable author of the plays is a tribute to the regard in which the plays are held. Unfortunately for their claims, the documents that exist that provide evidence for the facts of Shakespeare's life tie him inextricably to the body of plays and poems that bear his name. Unlikely as it seems to those who want the works to have been written by an aristocrat, a university graduate, or an "important" person, the plays and poems seem clearly to have been produced by a man from Stratford-upon-Avon with a very good "grammar-school" education and a life of experience in London and in the world of the London theater. How this particular man produced the works that dominate the cultures of much of the world almost four hundred years after his death is one of life's mysteries—and one that will continue to tease our imaginations as we continue to delight in his plays and poems.

Shakespeare's Theater

The actors of Shakespeare's time are known to have performed plays in a great variety of locations. They played at court (that is, in the great halls of such royal residences as Whitehall, Hampton Court, and Greenwich); they played in halls at the universities of Oxford and Cambridge, and at the Inns of Court (the residences in London of the legal societies); and they also played in the private houses of great lords and civic officials. Sometimes acting companies went on tour from London into the provinces, often (but not only) when outbreaks of bubonic plague in the capital forced the closing of theaters to reduce the possibility of contagion in crowded audiences. In the provinces the actors usually staged their plays in churches (until around 1600) or in guildhalls. While surviving records show only a handful of occasions when actors played at inns while on tour, London inns were important playing-places up until the 1590s.

The building of theaters in London had begun only shortly before Shakespeare wrote his first plays in the 1590s. These theaters were of two kinds: outdoor or public playhouses that could accommodate large numbers of playgoers, and indoor or private theaters for much smaller audiences. What is usually regarded as the first London outdoor public playhouse was called simply the Theatre. James Burbage, the father of Richard Burbage, who was perhaps the most famous actor in Shakespeare's company, built it in 1576 in an area of the city of London called Shoreditch. Among the more famous of the other public playhouses that capitalized on the new fashion were the Curtain and the Fortune (both also built north of the city), the Rose, the Swan, the Globe, and the Hope (all located on the Bankside, a region just across the Thames south of the city of London). All these playhouses had to be built outside the jurisdiction of the city of London because many civic officials were hostile to the performance of drama and repeatedly petitioned the royal council to abolish it.

The theaters erected on the Bankside (a region under the authority of the Church of England, whose head was the monarch) shared the neighborhood with houses of prostitution and with the Paris Garden, where the blood sports of bearbaiting and bullbaiting were carried on. There may have been no clear distinction between playhouses and buildings for such sports, for we know that the Hope was used for both plays and baiting and that Philip Henslowe, owner of the Rose and, later, partner in the ownership of the Fortune, was also a partner in a monopoly on baiting. All these forms of entertainment were easily accessible to Londoners by boat across the Thames or over London Bridge.

Evidently Shakespeare's company prospered on the Bankside. They moved there in 1599. Threatened by difficulties in renewing the lease on the land where their first theater (the Theatre) had been built, Shakespeare's company took advantage of the Christmas holiday in 1598 to dismantle the Theatre and transport its timbers across the Thames to the Bankside, where, in 1599, these timbers were used in the building of the Globe. The weather in late December 1598 is recorded as having been especially harsh. It was so cold that the Thames was "nigh [nearly] frozen," and there was heavy snow. Perhaps the weather aided Shakespeare's company in eluding their landlord, the snow hiding their activity and the freezing of the Thames allowing them to slide the timbers across to the Bankside without paying tolls for repeated trips over London Bridge. Attractive as this narrative is, it remains just as likely that the heavy snow hampered transport of the timbers in wagons through the London streets to the river. It also must be remembered that the Thames was, according to report, only "nigh frozen" and therefore as impassable as it ever was. Whatever the precise circumstances of this fascinating event in English theater history, Shakespeare's company was able to begin playing at their new Globe theater on the Bankside in 1599. After the first Globe burned down in 1613 during the staging of Shakespeare's *Henry VIII* (its thatch roof was set alight by cannon fire called for in the playtext), Shakespeare's company immediately rebuilt on the same location. The second Globe seems to have been a grander structure than its predecessor. It remained in use until the beginning of the English Civil War in 1642, when Parliament officially closed the theaters. Soon thereafter it was pulled down.

The public theaters of Shakespeare's time were very different buildings from our theaters today. First of all, they were open-air playhouses. As recent excavations of the Rose and the Globe confirm, some were polygonal or roughly circular in shape; the Fortune, however, was square. The most recent estimates of their size put the diameter of these buildings at 72 feet (the Rose) to 100 feet (the Globe), but we know that they held vast audiences of two or three thousand, who must have been squeezed together quite tightly. Some of these spectators paid extra to sit or stand in the two or three levels of roofed galleries that extended, on the upper levels, all the way around the theater and surrounded an open space. In this space were the stage and, perhaps, the tiring house (what we would call dressing rooms), as well as the so-called yard. In the yard stood the spectators who chose to pay less, the ones whom Hamlet contemptuously called "groundlings." For a roof they had only the sky, and so they were exposed to all kinds of weather. They stood on a floor that was sometimes made of mortar and sometimes of ash mixed with the shells of hazelnuts. The latter provided a porous and therefore dry footing for the crowd, and the shells may have been more comfortable to stand on because they were not as hard as mortar. Availability of shells may not have been a problem if hazelnuts were a favorite food for Shakespeare's audiences to munch on as they watched his plays. Archaeologists who are today unearthing the remains of theaters from this period have discovered quantities of these nutshells on theater sites.

Unlike the yard, the stage itself was covered by a roof. Its ceiling, called "the heavens," is thought to have been elaborately painted to depict the sun, moon, stars, and planets. Just how big the stage was remains hard to determine. We have a single sketch of part of the interior of the Swan. A Dutchman named Johannes de Witt visited this theater around 1596 and sent a sketch of it back to his friend, Arend van Buchel. Because van Buchel found de Witt's letter and sketch of interest, he copied both into a book. It is van Buchel's copy, adapted, it seems, to the shape and size of the page in his book, that survives. In this sketch, the stage appears to be a large rectangular platform that thrusts far out into the yard, perhaps even as far as the center of the circle formed by the surrounding galleries. This drawing, combined with the specifications for the size of the stage in the building contract for the Fortune, has led scholars to conjecture that the stage on which Shakespeare's plays were performed must have measured approximately 43 feet in width and 27 feet in depth, a vast acting area. But the digging up of a large part of the Rose by archaeologists has provided evidence of a quite different stage design. The Rose stage was a platform tapered at the corners and much shallower than what seems to be depicted in the van Buchel sketch. Indeed, its measurements seem to be about 37.5 feet across at its widest point and only 15.5 feet deep. Because the surviving indications of stage size and design differ from each other so much, it is possible that the stages in other theaters, like the Theatre, the Curtain, and the Globe (the outdoor playhouses where we know that Shakespeare's plays were performed), were different from those at both the Swan and the Rose.

After about 1608 Shakespeare's plays were staged not only at the Globe but also at an indoor or private playhouse in Blackfriars. This theater had been constructed in 1596 by James Burbage in an upper hall of a former Dominican priory or monastic house. Although Henry VIII had dissolved all English monasteries in the 1530s (shortly after he had founded the Church of England), the area remained under church, rather than hostile civic, control. The hall that Burbage had purchased and renovated was a large one in which Parliament had once met. In the private theater that he constructed, the stage, lit by candles, was built across the narrow end of the hall, with boxes flanking it. The rest of the hall offered seating room only. Because there was no provision for standing room, the largest audience it could hold was less than a thousand, or about a quarter what the Globe could accommodate. Admission to Blackfriars was correspondingly more expensive. Instead of a penny to stand in the yard at the Globe, it cost a minimum of sixpence to get into Blackfriars. The best seats at the Globe (in the Lords' Room in the gallery above and behind the stage) cost sixpence; but the boxes flanking the stage at Blackfriars were half a crown, or five times sixpence. Some spectators who were particularly interested in displaying themselves paid even more to sit on stools on the Blackfriars stage.

Whether in the outdoor or indoor playhouses, the stages of Shakespeare's time were different from ours. They were not separated from the audience by the dropping of a curtain between acts and scenes. Therefore the playwrights of the time had to find other ways of signaling to the audience that one scene (to be imagined as occurring in one location at a given time) had ended and the next (to be imagined at perhaps a different location at a later time) had begun. The customary way used by Shakespeare and many of his contemporaries was to have everyone onstage exit at the end of one scene and have one or more different characters enter to begin the next. In a few cases, where characters remain onstage from one scene to another, the dialogue or stage action makes the change of location clear, and the characters are generally to be imagined as having moved from one place to another. For example, in *Romeo and Juliet*, Romeo and his friends remain onstage in Act 1 from scene 4 to scene 5, but they are represented as having moved between scenes from the street that leads to Capulet's house into Capulet's house itself. The new location is signaled in part by the appearance onstage of Capulet's servingmen carrying napkins, something they would not take into the streets. Playwrights had to be quite resourceful in the use of hand properties, like the napkin, or in the use of dialogue to specify where the action was taking place in their plays because, in contrast to most of today's theaters, the playhouses of Shakespeare's time did not use movable scenery to dress the stage and make the setting precise. As another consequence of this difference, however, the playwrights of Shakespeare's time did not have to specify exactly where the action of their plays was set when they did not choose to do so, and much of the action of their plays is tied to no specific place.

Usually Shakespeare's stage is referred to as a "bare stage," to distinguish it from the stages of the last two or three centuries with their elaborate sets. But the stage in Shakespeare's time was not completely bare. Philip Henslowe, owner of the Rose, lists in his inventory of stage properties a rock, three tombs, and two mossy banks. Stage directions in plays of the time also call for such things as thrones (or "states"), banquets (presumably tables with plaster replicas of food on them), and beds and tombs to be pushed onto the stage. Thus the stage often held more than the actors.

The actors did not limit their performing to the stage alone. Occasionally they went beneath the stage, as the Ghost appears to do in the first act of *Hamlet*. From there they could emerge onto the stage through a trapdoor. They could retire behind the hangings across the back of the stage (or the front of the tiring house), as, for example, the actor playing Polonius does when he hides behind the arras. Sometimes the hangings could be drawn back during a performance to "discover" one or more actors behind them. When performance required that an actor appear "above," as when Juliet is imagined to stand at the window of her chamber in the famous and misnamed "balcony scene," then the actor probably climbed the stairs to the gallery over the back of the stage and temporarily shared it with some of the spectators. The stage was also provided with ropes and winches so that actors could descend from, and reascend to, the "heavens."

Perhaps the greatest difference between dramatic performances in Shakespeare's time and ours was that in Shakespeare's England the roles of women were played by boys. (Some of these boys grew up to take male roles in their maturity.) There were no women in the acting companies, only in the audience. It had not always been so in the history of the English stage. There are records of women on English stages in the thirteenth and fourteenth centuries, two hundred years before Shakespeare's plays were performed. After the accession of James I in 1603, the queen of England and her ladies took part in entertainments at court called masques, and with the reopening of the theaters in 1660 at the restoration of Charles II, women again took their place on the public stage.

The chief competitors for the companies of adult actors such as the one to which Shakespeare belonged and for which he wrote were companies of exclusively boy actors. The competition was most intense in the early 1600s. There were then two principal children's companies: the Children of Paul's (the choirboys from St. Paul's Cathedral, whose private playhouse was near the cathedral); and the Children of the Chapel Royal (the choirboys from the monarch's private chapel, who performed at the Blackfriars theater built by Burbage in 1596, which Shakespeare's company had been stopped from using by local residents who objected to crowds). In *Hamlet* Shakespeare writes of "an aerie [nest] of children, little eyases [hawks], that cry out on the top of question and are most tyrannically clapped for 't. These are now the fashion and . . . berattle the common stages [attack the public theaters]." In the long run, the adult actors prevailed. The Children of Paul's dissolved around 1606. By about 1608 the Children of the Chapel Royal had been forced to stop playing at the Blackfriars theater, which was then taken over by the King's Men, Shakespeare's own troupe.

Acting companies and theaters of Shakespeare's time were organized in different ways. For example, Philip Henslowe owned the Rose and leased it to companies of actors, who paid him from their takings. Henslowe would act as manager of these companies, initially paying playwrights for their plays and buying properties, recovering his outlay from the actors. Shakespeare's company, however, managed itself, with the principal actors, Shakespeare among them, having the status of "sharers" and the right to a share in the takings, as well as the responsibility for a part of the expenses. Five of the sharers themselves, Shakespeare among them, owned the Globe. As actor, as sharer in an acting company and in ownership of theaters, and as playwright, Shakespeare was about as involved in the theatrical industry as one could imagine. Although Shakespeare and his fellows prospered, their status under the law was conditional upon the protection of powerful patrons. "Common players"—those who did not have patrons or masters—were classed in the language of the law with "vagabonds and sturdy beggars." So the actors had to secure for themselves the official rank of servants of patrons. Among the patrons under whose protection Shakespeare's company worked were the lord chamberlain and, after the accession of King James in 1603, the king himself.

We are now perhaps on the verge of learning a great deal more about the theaters in which Shakespeare and his contemporaries performed—or at least of opening up new questions about them. Already about 70 percent of the Rose has been excavated, as has about 10 percent of the second Globe, the one built in 1614. It is to be hoped that soon more will be available for study. These are exciting times for students of Shakespeare's stage.

The Publication of Shakespeare's Plays

Eighteen of Shakespeare's plays found their way into print during the playwright's lifetime, but there is nothing to suggest that he took any interest in their publication. These eighteen appeared separately in editions called quartos. Their pages were not much larger than the one you are now reading, and these little books were sold unbound for a few pence. The earliest of the quartos that still survive were printed in 1594, the year that both *Titus Andronicus* and a version of the play now called *King Henry VI* became available. While almost every one of these early quartos displays on its title page the name of the acting company that performed the play, only about half provide the name of the playwright, Shakespeare. The first quarto edition to bear the name Shakespeare on its title page is *Love's Labor's Lost* of 1598. A few of these quartos were popular with the book-buying public of Shakespeare's lifetime; for example, quarto *Richard II* went through five editions between 1597 and 1615. But most of the quartos were far from best-sellers; *Love's Labor's Lost* (1598), for instance, was not reprinted in quarto until 1631. After Shakespeare's death, two more of his plays appeared in quarto format: *Othello* in 1622 and *The Two Noble Kinsmen*, coauthored with John Fletcher, in 1634.

In 1623, seven years after Shakespeare's death, was published *Mr. William Shakespeares Comedies, Histories, & Tragedies*. This printing offered readers in a single book thirty-six of the thirty-eight plays now thought to have been written by Shakespeare, including eighteen that had never been printed before. And it offered them in a style that was then reserved for serious literature and scholarship. The plays were arranged in double columns on pages nearly a foot high. This large page size is called "folio," as opposed to the smaller "quarto," and the 1623 volume is usually called the Shakespeare First Folio. It is reputed to have sold for the lordly price of a pound. (One copy at the Folger Library is marked fifteen shillings—that is, three-quarters of a pound.)

In a preface to the First Folio entitled "To the great Variety of Readers," two of Shakespeare's former fellow actors in the King's Men, John Heminge and Henry Condell, wrote that they themselves had collected their dead companion's plays. They suggested that they had seen his own papers: "we have scarce received from him a blot in his papers." The title page of the Folio declared that the plays within it had been printed "according to the True Original Copies." Comparing the Folio to the quartos, Heminge and Condell disparaged the quartos, advising their readers that "before you were abused with divers stolen and surreptitious copies, maimed, and deformed by the frauds and stealths of injurious impostors." Many Shakespeareans of the eighteenth and nineteenth centuries believed Heminge and Condell and regarded the Folio plays as superior to anything in the quartos.

Once we begin to examine the Folio plays in detail, it becomes less easy to take at face value the word of Heminge and Condell about the superiority of the Folio texts. For example, of the first nine plays in the Folio (one quarter of the entire collection), four were essentially reprinted from earlier quarto printings that Heminge and Condell had disparaged; and four have now been identified as printed from copies written in the hand of a professional scribe of the 1620s named Ralph Crane; the ninth, *The Comedy of Errors,* was apparently also printed from a manuscript, but one whose origin cannot be readily identified. Evidently then, eight of the first nine plays in the First Folio were not printed, in spite of what the Folio title page announces, "according to the True Originall Copies" or Shakespeare's own papers, and the source of the ninth is unknown. Since today's editors have been forced to treat Heminge and Condell's pronouncements with skepticism, they must choose whether to base their own editions upon quartos or the Folio on grounds other than Heminge and Condell's story of where the quarto and Folio versions originated.

Editors have often fashioned their own narratives to explain what lies behind the quartos and Folio. They have said that Heminge and Condell meant to criticize only a few of the early quartos, the ones that offer much shorter and sometimes quite different, often garbled, versions of plays. Among the examples of these are the 1600 quarto of *Henry V* (the Folio offers a much fuller version) or the 1603 *Hamlet* quarto (in 1604 a different, much longer form of the play got into print as a quarto). Early in this century editors speculated that these questionable texts were produced when someone in the audience took notes from the plays' dialogue during performances and then employed "hack poets" to fill out the notes. The poor results were then sold to a publisher and presented in print as Shakespeare's plays. More recently this story has given way to another in which the shorter versions are said to be recreations from memory of Shakespeare's plays by actors who wanted to stage them in the provinces but lacked manuscript copies. Most of the quartos offer much better texts than these so-called bad quartos. Indeed, in most of the quartos we find texts that are at least equal to or better than what is printed in the Folio. Many of this century's Shakespeare enthusiasts have persuaded themselves that most of the quartos were set into type directly from Shakespeare's own papers, although there is nothing on which to base this conclusion except the desire for it to be true. Thus speculation continues about how the Shakespeare plays got to be printed. All that we have are the printed texts.

The book collector who was most successful in bringing together copies of the quartos and the First Folio was Henry Clay Folger, founder of the Folger Shakespeare Library in Washington, D.C. While it is estimated that there survive around the world only about 230 copies of the First Folio, Mr. Folger was able to acquire more than seventy-five copies, as well as a large number of fragments, for the library that bears his name. He also amassed a substantial number of quartos. For example, only fourteen copies of the First Quarto of *Love's Labor's Lost* are known to exist, and three are at the Folger Shakespeare Library. As a consequence of Mr. Folger's labors, twentieth-century scholars visiting the Folger Library have been able to learn a great deal about sixteenth- and seventeenth-century printing and, particularly, about the printing of Shakespeare's plays. And Mr. Folger did not stop at the First Folio, but collected many copies of later editions of Shakespeare, beginning with the Second Folio (1632), the Third (1663–64), and the Fourth (1685). Each of these later folios was based on its immediate predecessor and was edited anonymously. The first editor of Shakespeare whose name we know was Nicholas Rowe, whose first edition came out in 1709. Mr. Folger collected this edition and many, many more by Rowe's successors.

An Introduction to This Text

Macbeth was first printed in the First Folio of 1623. The present edition is based directly upon that printing.* For the convenience of the reader, we have modernized the punctuation and the spelling of the First Folio. Sometimes we go so far as to modernize certain old forms of words; for example, when *a* means "he," we change it to *he;* we change *mo* to *more* and *ye* to *you.* But it is not our practice in editing any of the plays to modernize forms of words that sound distinctly different from modern forms. For example, when the early printed text reads *sith* or *apricocks* or *porpentine,* we have not modernized to *since, apricots, porcupine.* When the forms *an, and,* or *and if* appear instead of the modern form *if,* we have reduced *and* to *an* but have not changed any of these forms to their modern equivalent, *if.* We also modernize *and,* where necessary, correct passages in foreign languages, unless an error in the early printed text can be reasonably explained as a joke.

Whenever we change the wording of the First Folio or add anything to its stage directions, we mark the change by enclosing it in superior half-brackets (⌐¬). We want our readers to be immediately aware when we have intervened. (Only when we correct an obvious typographical error in the First Folio does the change not get marked.) Whenever we change the First Folio's wording or change its punctuation so that the meaning changes, we list the change in the textual notes at the back of the book, even if all we have done is fix an obvious error.

---

*We have also consulted the computerized text of the First Folio provided by the Text Archive of the Oxford University Computing Centre, to which we are grateful.

We correct or regularize a number of the proper
names, as is the usual practice in editions of the play. For
example, the Folio's occasional spelling "Dunsmane" is
altered to "Dunsinane," the Folio's more usual spelling,
and the various Folio spellings of Birnam Wood—
"Byrnam," "Byrnan," "Birnan," "Byrnane," and "Bir-
nane"—are all spelled "Birnam" in this edition. Since
no scholars believe that the Folio *Macbeth* was printed
directly from Shakespeare's own papers, it would be
difficult to identify the Folio's spellings of names as
Shakespeare's preferences.

This edition differs from many earlier ones in its
efforts to aid the reader in imagining the play as a
performance, rather than as a series of historical events.
Thus stage directions are written with reference to the
stage. For example, at 2.3.20, instead of providing a stage
direction that says "The Porter opens the gate," as many
editions do, this edition has "The Porter opens the
door." There may have been doors on Shakespeare's
stages for the Porter to open, but almost certainly there
were no gates.

Whenever it is reasonably certain, in our view, that a
speech is accompanied by a particular action, we provide a stage direction describing the action. (Occasional
exceptions to this rule occur when the action is so
obvious that to add a stage direction would insult the
reader.) Stage directions for the entrance of characters
in mid-scene are, with rare exceptions, placed so that
they immediately precede the characters' participation
in the scene, even though these entrances may appear
somewhat earlier in the early printed texts. Whenever
we move a stage direction, we record this change in the
textual notes. Latin stage directions (e.g., *Exeunt*) are
translated into English (e.g., *They exit*).

We expand the often severely abbreviated forms of
names used as speech headings in early printed texts

into the full names of the characters. We also regularize the speakers' names in speech headings, using only a single designation for each character, even though the early printed texts sometimes use a variety of designations. Variations in the speech headings of the early printed texts are recorded in the textual notes.

In the present edition, as well, we mark with a dash any change of address within a speech, unless a stage direction intervenes. When the *-ed* ending of a word is to be pronounced, we mark it with an accent. Like editors for the last two centuries, we print metrically linked lines in the following way:

MACBETH
  We will speak further.
LADY MACBETH   Only look up clear.

However, when there are a number of short verse-lines that can be linked in more than one way, we do not, with rare exceptions, indent any of them.

The Explanatory Notes

The notes that appear on the pages facing the text are designed to provide readers with the help that they may need to enjoy the play. Whenever the meaning of a word in the text is not readily accessible in a good contemporary dictionary, we offer the meaning in a note. Sometimes we provide a note even when the relevant meaning is to be found in the dictionary but when the word has acquired since Shakespeare's time other potentially confusing meanings. In our notes, we try to offer modern synonyms for Shakespeare's words. We also try to indicate to the reader the connection between the word in the play and the modern synonym. For example,

Shakespeare sometimes uses the word *head* to mean "source," but, for modern readers, there may be no connection evident between these two words. We provide the connection by explaining Shakespeare's usage as follows: **"head:** fountainhead, source." On some occasions, a whole phrase or clause needs explanation. Then we rephrase in our own words the difficult passage, and add at the end synonyms for individual words in the passage. When scholars have been unable to determine the meaning of a word or phrase, we acknowledge the uncertainty.

The Tragedy of

MACBETH

Characters in the Play

Three Witches, the Weïrd Sisters

DUNCAN, king of Scotland
MALCOLM, his elder son
DONALBAIN, Duncan's younger son

MACBETH, thane of Glamis
LADY MACBETH
SEYTON, attendant to Macbeth
Three Murderers in Macbeth's service
A Doctor ⎱ *both attending upon Lady Macbeth*
A Gentlewoman ⎰
A Porter

BANQUO, commander, with Macbeth, of Duncan's army
FLEANCE, his son

MACDUFF, a Scottish noble
LADY MACDUFF
Their son

LENNOX
ROSS
ANGUS ⎬ *Scottish nobles*
MENTEITH
CAITHNESS

SIWARD, commander of the English forces
YOUNG SIWARD, Siward's son

A Captain in Duncan's army
An Old Man
A Doctor at the English court

3

HECATE

Apparitions: an Armed Head, a Bloody Child, a Crowned Child, and eight nonspeaking kings

Three Messengers, Three Servants, a Lord, a Soldier

Attendants, a Sewer, Servants, Lords, Thanes, Soldiers (all nonspeaking)

The Tragedy of

MACBETH

ACT 1

1.1 Three witches plan to meet Macbeth.

---

3. **hurly-burly:** commotion

5. **ere:** before

9. **Graymalkin:** the name of the first witch's "familiar" (an attendant spirit serving her in the form of a cat)

10. **Paddock:** a toad, the "familiar" of the second witch

11. **Anon:** immediately (perhaps, the response of the third witch to her "familiar")

ACT 1

Scene 1
Thunder and lightning. Enter three Witches.

FIRST WITCH
When shall we three meet again?
In thunder, lightning, or in rain?
SECOND WITCH
When the hurly-burly's done,
When the battle's lost and won.
THIRD WITCH
That will be ere the set of sun.   5
FIRST WITCH
Where the place?
SECOND WITCH   Upon the heath.
THIRD WITCH
There to meet with Macbeth.
FIRST WITCH   I come, Graymalkin.
⌐SECOND WITCH⌐   Paddock calls.   10
⌐THIRD WITCH⌐   Anon.
ALL
Fair is foul, and foul is fair,
Hover through the fog and filthy air.
                                                    They exit.

1.2 Duncan, king of Scotland, hears an account of the success in battle of his noblemen Macbeth and Banquo. Duncan orders the execution of the rebel thane of Cawdor and sends messengers to announce to Macbeth that he has been given Cawdor's title.

———————

0 SD. **Alarum:** a trumpet "call to arms"

4. **sergeant:** soldier, officer (also called *Captain* in the Folio stage directions and speech prefixes)

7. **broil:** battle

10. **spent:** exhausted

11. **choke their art:** prevent each other from using their skill (in swimming)   **art:** skill

12. **to that:** to make him that (i.e., a rebel)

13. **villainies:** shameful evils

14. **Western Isles:** the Hebrides (islands off the west coast of Scotland)

15. **kerns and gallowglasses:** lightly armed undisciplined foot soldiers and soldiers heavily armed and well trained (The terms were usually applied to Irish soldiers.)

16. **damnèd quarrel:** the accursed cause (for which he fought)

17. **Showed . . . whore:** appeared to have granted the rebellious Macdonwald her favors; **all:** everything that Macdonwald and Fortune can do

21. **valor's minion:** the chosen darling of Valor

22. **slave:** villain (i.e., Macdonwald)

24. **unseamed . . . chops:** ripped him open from his navel to his jaw

27. **his reflection:** its apparent backward turning

Scene 2
Alarum within. Enter King ⌐Duncan,¬ Malcolm,
Donalbain, Lennox, with Attendants, meeting a bleeding
Captain.

DUNCAN
 What bloody man is that? He can report,
 As seemeth by his plight, of the revolt
 The newest state.
MALCOLM   This is the sergeant
 Who, like a good and hardy soldier, fought   5
 'Gainst my captivity.—Hail, brave friend!
 Say to the King the knowledge of the broil
 As thou didst leave it.
CAPTAIN   Doubtful it stood,
 As two spent swimmers that do cling together   10
 And choke their art. The merciless Macdonwald
 (Worthy to be a rebel, for to that
 The multiplying villainies of nature
 Do swarm upon him) from the Western Isles
 Of kerns and ⌐gallowglasses¬ is supplied;   15
 And Fortune, on his damnèd ⌐quarrel¬ smiling,
 Showed like a rebel's whore. But all's too weak;
 For brave Macbeth (well he deserves that name),
 Disdaining Fortune, with his brandished steel,
 Which smoked with bloody execution,   20
 Like valor's minion, carved out his passage
 Till he faced the slave;
 Which ne'er shook hands, nor bade farewell to him,
 Till he unseamed him from the nave to th' chops,
 And fixed his head upon our battlements.   25
DUNCAN
 O valiant cousin, worthy gentleman!
CAPTAIN
 As whence the sun 'gins his reflection
 Shipwracking storms and direful thunders ⌐break,¬

34. **the Norweyan lord:** i.e., the king of Norway; **surveying vantage:** seeing his chance

40. **say sooth:** speak truthfully

41. **cracks:** i.e., explosive charges

43. **Except:** unless

44. **memorize another Golgotha:** make the event (or place) memorable by turning it into a second Golgotha **Golgotha:** "the place of dead men's skulls" (Mark 15.22) where Jesus was crucified

48. **smack:** have the flavor, taste

50. **Thane:** a title used in Scotland as the equivalent of "baron"

52. **should:** is likely to

Golgotha. (1.2.44)
From Martin Luther, *Ein Sermon* (1523).

So from that spring whence comfort seemed to
   come   30
Discomfort swells. Mark, King of Scotland, mark:
No sooner justice had, with valor armed,
Compelled these skipping kerns to trust their heels,
But the Norweyan lord, surveying vantage,
With furbished arms and new supplies of men,   35
Began a fresh assault.
DUNCAN
Dismayed not this our captains, Macbeth and
   Banquo?
CAPTAIN
Yes, as sparrows eagles, or the hare the lion.
If I say sooth, I must report they were   40
As cannons overcharged with double cracks,
So they doubly redoubled strokes upon the foe.
Except they meant to bathe in reeking wounds
Or memorize another Golgotha,
I cannot tell—   45
But I am faint. My gashes cry for help.
DUNCAN
So well thy words become thee as thy wounds:
They smack of honor both.—Go, get him surgeons.
        ⌜*The Captain is led off by Attendants.*⌝

       Enter Ross and Angus.

Who comes here?
MALCOLM   The worthy Thane of Ross.   50
LENNOX
What a haste looks through his eyes!
So should he look that seems to speak things
   strange.
ROSS   God save the King.
DUNCAN   Whence cam'st thou, worthy thane?   55
ROSS   From Fife, great king,
Where the Norweyan banners flout the sky

58. **people:** i.e., troops

59. **Norway himself:** i.e., the king of Norway

61. **dismal:** ominous

62. **Bellona:** Roman goddess of war (Her bride-groom would be the fiercest of warriors.); **lapped in proof:** dressed in proven armor

63. **him:** the king of Norway; **self-comparisons:** (attacks) that matched his own

65. **lavish:** unrestrained

69. **Norways':** Norwegians'; **craves composition:** asks for terms

71. **Saint Colme's Inch:** i.e., Inchcolm, a small island in the Firth of Forth   **Colme's:** pronounced "kollums"

73–74. **deceive / Our bosom interest:** betray my dearest concerns   **Our:** i.e., my (the royal "we")

74. **present:** immediate

1.3   The three witches greet Macbeth as "Thane of Glamis" (as he is), "Thane of Cawdor," and "king hereafter." They then promise Banquo that he will father kings, and they disappear. Almost as soon as they are gone, Ross and Angus arrive with news that the king has named Macbeth "Thane of Cawdor." Macbeth contemplates killing Duncan in order to become "king hereafter" as the witches have called him.

———

7. **Aroint thee:** begone; **rump-fed:** fed on rump meat; fat-rumped; **runnion:** perhaps "scabby wom-an" or "fat woman"

And fan our people cold.
Norway himself, with terrible numbers,
Assisted by that most disloyal traitor,   60
The Thane of Cawdor, began a dismal conflict,
Till that Bellona's bridegroom, lapped in proof,
Confronted him with self-comparisons,
Point against point, rebellious arm 'gainst arm,
Curbing his lavish spirit. And to conclude,   65
The victory fell on us.
DUNCAN   Great happiness!
ROSS   That now Sweno,
The Norways' king, craves composition.
Nor would we deign him burial of his men   70
Till he disbursèd at Saint Colme's Inch
Ten thousand dollars to our general use.
DUNCAN
No more that Thane of Cawdor shall deceive
Our bosom interest. Go, pronounce his present
    death,   75
And with his former title greet Macbeth.
ROSS   I'll see it done.
DUNCAN
What he hath lost, noble Macbeth hath won.
                                            They exit.

                          Scene 3
            Thunder. Enter the three Witches.

FIRST WITCH   Where hast thou been, sister?
SECOND WITCH   Killing swine.
THIRD WITCH   Sister, where thou?
FIRST WITCH
A sailor's wife had chestnuts in her lap
And munched and munched and munched. "Give   5
    me," quoth I.
"Aroint thee, witch," the rump-fed runnion cries.

8. **Tiger:** the name of the sailor's ship

10. **like:** in the form of

15. **the other:** i.e., the other winds

16. **And . . . blow:** and (I have) the ports from which the winds blow

17. **quarters:** i.e., directions

18. **card:** compass card

21. **penthouse lid:** eyelid

22. **forbid:** under a curse

25. **bark:** ship; **lost:** destroyed

29. **pilot:** helmsman

30. **Wracked:** wrecked; also, tormented

33. **Weïrd:** fateful, fate-determining (In the Folio, the spelling is "weyward" or "weyard.") **Weïrd** is the Scottish form of *wyrd*, the Old English word for fate or destiny.

34. **Posters:** those who post, i.e., travel rapidly

Her husband's to Aleppo gone, master o' th' *Tiger;*
But in a sieve I'll thither sail,
And, like a rat without a tail,   10
I'll do, I'll do, and I'll do.
SECOND WITCH
    I'll give thee a wind.
FIRST WITCH
    Th' art kind.
THIRD WITCH
    And I another.
FIRST WITCH
    I myself have all the other,   15
    And the very ports they blow,
    All the quarters that they know
    I' th' shipman's card.
    I'll drain him dry as hay.
    Sleep shall neither night nor day   20
    Hang upon his penthouse lid.
    He shall live a man forbid.
    Weary sev'nnights, nine times nine,
    Shall he dwindle, peak, and pine.
    Though his bark cannot be lost,   25
    Yet it shall be tempest-tossed.
    Look what I have.
SECOND WITCH   Show me, show me.
FIRST WITCH
    Here I have a pilot's thumb,
    Wracked as homeward he did come.   *Drum within.*   30
THIRD WITCH
    A drum, a drum!
    Macbeth doth come.
ALL, ⌜*dancing in a circle*⌝
    The Weïrd Sisters, hand in hand,
    Posters of the sea and land,
    Thus do go about, about,   35
    Thrice to thine and thrice to mine

38. **wound up:** coiled (i.e., like a spring ready for action)

39. **have not seen:** have never seen before

40. **is 't called:** is it said to be

46. **choppy:** chapped; or, deeply wrinkled

47. **should be:** must be (i.e., most of your features indicate that you are)

56. **fantastical:** figments of the imagination

58. **present grace:** i.e., the title of "Thane of Glamis," already possessed by Macbeth

59. **noble having:** i.e., possession of noble titles; **royal hope:** hope of royal status

60. **That he seems rapt withal:** so that he seems transported by it all

63–64. **neither . . . hate:** neither beg your favors nor fear your hate

And thrice again, to make up nine.
Peace, the charm's wound up.

Enter Macbeth and Banquo.

MACBETH
So foul and fair a day I have not seen.
BANQUO
How far is 't called to ⌜Forres?⌝—What are these,   40
So withered, and so wild in their attire,
That look not like th' inhabitants o' th' earth
And yet are on 't?—Live you? Or are you aught
That man may question? You seem to understand
    me   45
By each at once her choppy finger laying
Upon her skinny lips. You should be women,
And yet your beards forbid me to interpret
That you are so.
MACBETH   Speak if you can. What are you?   50
FIRST WITCH
All hail, Macbeth! Hail to thee, Thane of Glamis!
SECOND WITCH
All hail, Macbeth! Hail to thee, Thane of Cawdor!
THIRD WITCH
All hail, Macbeth, that shalt be king hereafter!
BANQUO
Good sir, why do you start and seem to fear
Things that do sound so fair?—I' th' name of truth,   55
Are you fantastical, or that indeed
Which outwardly you show? My noble partner
You greet with present grace and great prediction
Of noble having and of royal hope,
That he seems rapt withal. To me you speak not.   60
If you can look into the seeds of time
And say which grain will grow and which will not,
Speak, then, to me, who neither beg nor fear
Your favors nor your hate.

69. **happy:** fortunate
70. **get:** beget, father
74. **Sinel:** Macbeth's father
79. **owe:** own
87. **insane root:** plant that causes insanity

Macbeth and Banquo meet the witches. (1.3.40–81)
From Raphael Holinshed, *The historie of Scotland* (1577).

FIRST WITCH Hail! 65
SECOND WITCH Hail!
THIRD WITCH Hail!
FIRST WITCH
  Lesser than Macbeth and greater.
SECOND WITCH
  Not so happy, yet much happier.
THIRD WITCH
  Thou shalt get kings, though thou be none. 70
  So all hail, Macbeth and Banquo!
FIRST WITCH
  Banquo and Macbeth, all hail!
MACBETH
  Stay, you imperfect speakers. Tell me more.
  By Sinel's death I know I am Thane of Glamis.
  But how of Cawdor? The Thane of Cawdor lives 75
  A prosperous gentleman, and to be king
  Stands not within the prospect of belief,
  No more than to be Cawdor. Say from whence
  You owe this strange intelligence or why
  Upon this blasted heath you stop our way 80
  With such prophetic greeting. Speak, I charge you.
                              Witches vanish.
BANQUO
  The earth hath bubbles, as the water has,
  And these are of them. Whither are they vanished?
MACBETH
  Into the air, and what seemed corporal melted,
  As breath into the wind. Would they had stayed! 85
BANQUO
  Were such things here as we do speak about?
  Or have we eaten on the insane root
  That takes the reason prisoner?
MACBETH
  Your children shall be kings.
BANQUO   You shall be king. 90

93. **happily:** with satisfaction

96–97. **His wonders . . . his:** i.e., the wonder he feels, which makes him speechless, vies with his desire to offer praise (Since he is **silenced** [line 97], his wonder wins the battle.)

101–2. **As thick . . . post:** couriers arrived as rapidly as they could be counted   **tale:** count

109. **earnest:** a small payment to seal a bargain; thus, a promise of a greater reward to come

111. **addition:** title

116. **Who:** he who

119. **combined:** in conspiracy

MACBETH
  And Thane of Cawdor too. Went it not so?
BANQUO
  To th' selfsame tune and words.—Who's here?

Enter Ross and Angus.

ROSS
  The King hath happily received, Macbeth,
  The news of thy success, and, when he reads
  Thy personal venture in the rebels' fight,   95
  His wonders and his praises do contend
  Which should be thine or his. Silenced with that,
  In viewing o'er the rest o' th' selfsame day
  He finds thee in the stout Norweyan ranks,
  Nothing afeard of what thyself didst make,   100
  Strange images of death. As thick as tale
  ⌈Came⌉ post with post, and every one did bear
  Thy praises in his kingdom's great defense,
  And poured them down before him.
ANGUS   We are sent   105
  To give thee from our royal master thanks,
  Only to herald thee into his sight,
  Not pay thee.
ROSS
  And for an earnest of a greater honor,
  He bade me, from him, call thee Thane of Cawdor,   110
  In which addition, hail, most worthy thane,
  For it is thine.
BANQUO   What, can the devil speak true?
MACBETH
  The Thane of Cawdor lives. Why do you dress me
  In borrowed robes?   115
ANGUS   Who was the Thane lives yet,
  But under heavy judgment bears that life
  Which he deserves to lose. Whether he was
    combined

120. **line the rebel:** i.e., reinforce Macdonwald

126. **The greatest is behind:** the greater part of the prophecy is already accomplished

132. **home:** i.e., fully

137. **betray 's:** betray us

141. **happy:** fortunate

143. **soliciting:** seduction, temptation

144. **ill:** evil

148. **unfix my hair:** make my hair stand on end

149. **seated:** i.e., fixed in its place

150. **Against . . . nature:** unnaturally **use:** custom; **Present fears:** causes of fear that are present

151. **horrible imaginings:** imaginary horrors

152. **fantastical:** imaginary

154. **function:** ability to act; **surmise:** speculation

155. **but:** except

With those of Norway, or did line the rebel   120
With hidden help and vantage, or that with both
He labored in his country's wrack, I know not;
But treasons capital, confessed and proved,
Have overthrown him.
MACBETH, ⌜*aside*⌝   Glamis and Thane of Cawdor!   125
  The greatest is behind. ⌜*To Ross and Angus.*⌝ Thanks
    for your pains.
  ⌜*Aside to Banquo.*⌝ Do you not hope your children
    shall be kings
  When those that gave the Thane of Cawdor to me   130
  Promised no less to them?
BANQUO   That, trusted home,
  Might yet enkindle you unto the crown,
  Besides the Thane of Cawdor. But 'tis strange.
  And oftentimes, to win us to our harm,   135
  The instruments of darkness tell us truths,
  Win us with honest trifles, to betray 's
  In deepest consequence.—
  Cousins, a word, I pray you.   ⌜*They step aside.*⌝
MACBETH, ⌜*aside*⌝   Two truths are told   140
  As happy prologues to the swelling act
  Of the imperial theme.—I thank you, gentlemen.
  ⌜*Aside.*⌝ This supernatural soliciting
  Cannot be ill, cannot be good. If ill,
  Why hath it given me earnest of success   145
  Commencing in a truth? I am Thane of Cawdor.
  If good, why do I yield to that suggestion
  Whose horrid image doth unfix my hair
  And make my seated heart knock at my ribs
  Against the use of nature? Present fears   150
  Are less than horrible imaginings.
  My thought, whose murder yet is but fantastical,
  Shakes so my single state of man
  That function is smothered in surmise,
  And nothing is but what is not.   155

159. **stir:** stirring; taking action

161. **our strange garments:** i.e., new clothes; **cleave . . . mold:** do not fit the body's form

162. **But:** except

172. **The interim having weighed it:** i.e., having thought about it in the interim

1.4 Duncan demands and receives assurances that the former thane of Cawdor has been executed. When Macbeth, Banquo, Ross, and Angus join Duncan, he offers thanks to Macbeth and Banquo. He then announces his intention to have his son Malcolm succeed him as king and his plan to visit Macbeth at Inverness. Macbeth sets out ahead of him to prepare for the royal visit. Now that Malcolm has been named Duncan's successor, Macbeth is convinced that he can become king only by killing Duncan.

---

0 SD. **Flourish:** fanfare of trumpets

2. **in commission:** i.e., commissioned (to carry out the execution)

BANQUO   Look how our partner's rapt.
MACBETH, ⌜*aside*⌝
  If chance will have me king, why, chance may
    crown me
  Without my stir.
BANQUO   New honors come upon him,   160
  Like our strange garments, cleave not to their mold
  But with the aid of use.
MACBETH, ⌜*aside*⌝   Come what come may,
  Time and the hour runs through the roughest day.
BANQUO
  Worthy Macbeth, we stay upon your leisure.   165
MACBETH
  Give me your favor. My dull brain was wrought
  With things forgotten. Kind gentlemen, your pains
  Are registered where every day I turn
  The leaf to read them. Let us toward the King.
  ⌜*Aside to Banquo.*⌝ Think upon what hath chanced,   170
    and at more time,
  The interim having weighed it, let us speak
  Our free hearts each to other.
BANQUO   Very gladly.
MACBETH   Till then enough.—Come, friends.   175
                                            They exit.

                        Scene 4
  Flourish. Enter King ⌜*Duncan,*⌝ *Lennox, Malcolm,*
            Donalbain, and Attendants.

DUNCAN
  Is execution done on Cawdor? ⌜Are⌝ not
  Those in commission yet returned?
MALCOLM   My liege,
  They are not yet come back. But I have spoke
  With one that saw him die, who did report   5

11. **owed:** owned

12. **careless:** uncared for, worthless

22–23. **That the proportion . . . mine:** that both my thanks and my payment might have exceeded what you deserve

24. **all:** i.e., all I possess

26. **pays itself:** i.e., is its own reward

27–28. **our duties . . . servants:** i.e., we, as dutiful subjects, owe to you the obligations that children owe parents and servants owe masters

30. **Safe toward:** protective of

Execution of a Scottish noble. (1.4.1–12)
From Raphael Holinshed, *The historie of Scotland* (1577).

That very frankly he confessed his treasons,
Implored your Highness' pardon, and set forth
A deep repentance. Nothing in his life
Became him like the leaving it. He died
As one that had been studied in his death   10
To throw away the dearest thing he owed
As 'twere a careless trifle.
DUNCAN   There's no art
To find the mind's construction in the face.
He was a gentleman on whom I built   15
An absolute trust.

     Enter Macbeth, Banquo, Ross, and Angus.

                O worthiest cousin,
The sin of my ingratitude even now
Was heavy on me. Thou art so far before
That swiftest wing of recompense is slow   20
To overtake thee. Would thou hadst less deserved,
That the proportion both of thanks and payment
Might have been mine! Only I have left to say,
More is thy due than more than all can pay.
MACBETH
The service and the loyalty I owe   25
In doing it pays itself. Your Highness' part
Is to receive our duties, and our duties
Are to your throne and state children and servants,
Which do but what they should by doing everything
Safe toward your love and honor.   30
DUNCAN   Welcome hither.
I have begun to plant thee and will labor
To make thee full of growing.—Noble Banquo,
That hast no less deserved nor must be known
No less to have done so, let me enfold thee   35
And hold thee to my heart.
BANQUO   There, if I grow,
The harvest is your own.

40. **Wanton:** unrestrained

43. **We . . . estate:** i.e., I name as my heir

44. **hereafter:** henceforth, from now on

45. **Prince of Cumberland:** heir to the throne

46. **Not . . . only:** i.e., not be bestowed on him without accompanying honors to others

48. **Inverness:** Macbeth's castle

50. **rest:** leisure, repose

51. **harbinger:** one who signals the approach of another

59. **The eye . . . hand:** i.e., let my eye not see what my hand does

61. **full so valiant:** perhaps, quite as valiant as you have said him to be (If this is the correct reading, Duncan is here responding to a comment made to him by Banquo during Macbeth's "aside.")

62. **his commendations:** the praises given him

64. **before:** ahead

DUNCAN   My plenteous joys,
  Wanton in fullness, seek to hide themselves   40
  In drops of sorrow.—Sons, kinsmen, thanes,
  And you whose places are the nearest, know
  We will establish our estate upon
  Our eldest, Malcolm, whom we name hereafter
  The Prince of Cumberland; which honor must   45
  Not unaccompanied invest him only,
  But signs of nobleness, like stars, shall shine
  On all deservers.—From hence to Inverness
  And bind us further to you.

MACBETH
  The rest is labor which is not used for you.   50
  I'll be myself the harbinger and make joyful
  The hearing of my wife with your approach.
  So humbly take my leave.

DUNCAN   My worthy Cawdor.

MACBETH, ⌐*aside*¬
  The Prince of Cumberland! That is a step   55
  On which I must fall down or else o'erleap,
  For in my way it lies. Stars, hide your fires;
  Let not light see my black and deep desires.
  The eye wink at the hand, yet let that be
  Which the eye fears, when it is done, to see.   60
                                 He exits.

DUNCAN
  True, worthy Banquo. He is full so valiant,
  And in his commendations I am fed:
  It is a banquet to me.—Let's after him,
  Whose care is gone before to bid us welcome.
  It is a peerless kinsman.   65
                                Flourish. They exit.

1.5   Lady Macbeth reads her husband's letter about his meeting the witches. She fears that Macbeth lacks the ruthlessness he needs to kill Duncan and fulfill the witches' second prophecy. When she learns that Duncan is coming to visit, she calls upon supernatural agents to fill her with cruelty. Macbeth arrives, and Lady Macbeth tells him that she will take charge of the preparations for Duncan's visit and for his murder.

---

12. **dues of rejoicing:** i.e., the due measure of joy

16. **fear:** worry about

18. **catch:** take; **wouldst:** wish to

20. **illness:** i.e., ruthlessness

20–21. **wouldst highly:** would greatly like (to have); also, would like to do ambitiously—or idealistically

22. **wouldst thou holily:** would like (to do) in a saintly way

23–28. **Thou'd'st . . . undone:** Lady Macbeth's avoidance of such terms as "murder" and "assassination" leads to imprecise use of **that** and **it.**

28. **should be undone:** i.e., should not be done

29. **spirits:** vital power, energy

30. **chastise:** rebuke; also, inflict punishment on

31. **round:** i.e., the crown

32. **metaphysical:** supernatural

33. **withal:** i.e., with

Scene 5
Enter Macbeth's Wife, alone, with a letter.

LADY MACBETH, ⌜*reading the letter*⌝ *They met me in the*
day of success, and I have learned by the perfect'st
report they have more in them than mortal knowledge.
When I burned in desire to question them further, they
made themselves air, into which they vanished.   5
Whiles I stood rapt in the wonder of it came missives
from the King, who all-hailed me "Thane of Cawdor,"
by which title, before, these Weïrd Sisters saluted me
and referred me to the coming on of time with "Hail,
king that shalt be." This have I thought good to deliver   10
thee, my dearest partner of greatness, that thou
might'st not lose the dues of rejoicing by being igno-
rant of what greatness is promised thee. Lay it to thy
heart, and farewell.
Glamis thou art, and Cawdor, and shalt be   15
What thou art promised. Yet do I fear thy nature;
It is too full o' th' milk of human kindness
To catch the nearest way. Thou wouldst be great,
Art not without ambition, but without
The illness should attend it. What thou wouldst   20
    highly,
That wouldst thou holily; wouldst not play false
And yet wouldst wrongly win. Thou'd'st have, great
    Glamis,
That which cries "Thus thou must do," if thou have   25
    it,
And that which rather thou dost fear to do,
Than wishest should be undone. Hie thee hither,
That I may pour my spirits in thine ear
And chastise with the valor of my tongue   30
All that impedes thee from the golden round,
Which fate and metaphysical aid doth seem
To have thee crowned withal.

37. **were 't so:** i.e., if the king were coming
38. **informed for preparation:** sent word so that we could be prepared
40. **had the speed of him:** outrode him
43. **Give him tending:** tend to (take care of) him
46. **fatal:** directed by fate; fatal to Duncan
48. **mortal:** deadly
49. **crown:** top of the head
51. **remorse:** compassion
52. **compunctious:** remorseful; **visitings:** promptings; **nature:** natural feelings
53. **fell:** cruel; deadly
53–54. **keep . . . it:** prevent my purpose from having its effect
55. **for gall:** in exchange for bile, the humor associated with envy and hatred; **ministers:** agents
56. **sightless:** invisible
57. **wait on:** attend; also, perhaps, lie in wait for, or accompany; **mischief:** evil
58. **pall thee:** cover yourself as with a pall, a dark cloth that is put over a coffin; **dunnest:** darkest
63. **all-hail hereafter:** i.e., future kingship

Enter Messenger.

What is your tidings?

MESSENGER
  The King comes here tonight.   35
LADY MACBETH   Thou 'rt mad to say it.
  Is not thy master with him, who, were 't so,
  Would have informed for preparation?
MESSENGER
  So please you, it is true. Our thane is coming.
  One of my fellows had the speed of him,   40
  Who, almost dead for breath, had scarcely more
  Than would make up his message.
LADY MACBETH   Give him tending.
  He brings great news.   *Messenger exits.*
                    The raven himself is hoarse   45
  That croaks the fatal entrance of Duncan
  Under my battlements. Come, you spirits
  That tend on mortal thoughts, unsex me here,
  And fill me from the crown to the toe top-full
  Of direst cruelty. Make thick my blood.   50
  Stop up th' access and passage to remorse,
  That no compunctious visitings of nature
  Shake my fell purpose, nor keep peace between
  Th' effect and it. Come to my woman's breasts
  And take my milk for gall, you murd'ring ministers,   55
  Wherever in your sightless substances
  You wait on nature's mischief. Come, thick night,
  And pall thee in the dunnest smoke of hell,
  That my keen knife see not the wound it makes,
  Nor heaven peep through the blanket of the dark   60
  To cry "Hold, hold!"

Enter Macbeth.

                    Great Glamis, worthy Cawdor,
  Greater than both by the all-hail hereafter!

65. **ignorant:** i.e., unaware of the future
66. **instant:** present moment
74. **beguile the time:** deceive those around us
80. **dispatch:** management (with a secondary sense of "putting to death")
82. **solely sovereign:** absolute; **sway:** power
85. **favor:** expression; **fear:** frighten

1.6 Duncan and his attendants arrive at Inverness. Lady Macbeth welcomes them.

---

0 SD. **Hautboys:** powerful double-reed woodwind instruments, also called "shawms," designed for outdoor ceremonials (Oboes are later descendants of hautboys, with a much softer tone, designed for use in orchestras.)

Hautboy. (1.6.0 SD)
From Balthasar Küchler, *Repraesentatio der fürstlichen Auffzug und Ritterspil* (1611).

Thy letters have transported me beyond
This ignorant present, and I feel now   65
The future in the instant.
MACBETH   My dearest love,
    Duncan comes here tonight.
LADY MACBETH   And when goes hence?
MACBETH
Tomorrow, as he purposes.   70
LADY MACBETH   O, never
    Shall sun that morrow see!
    Your face, my thane, is as a book where men
    May read strange matters. To beguile the time,
    Look like the time. Bear welcome in your eye,   75
    Your hand, your tongue. Look like th' innocent
        flower,
    But be the serpent under 't. He that's coming
    Must be provided for; and you shall put
    This night's great business into my dispatch,   80
    Which shall to all our nights and days to come
    Give solely sovereign sway and masterdom.
MACBETH
    We will speak further.
LADY MACBETH   Only look up clear.
    To alter favor ever is to fear.   85
    Leave all the rest to me.
                                          They exit.

                        Scene 6
Hautboys and Torches. Enter King ⌜Duncan,⌝ Malcolm,
Donalbain, Banquo, Lennox, Macduff, Ross, Angus, and
                        Attendants.

DUNCAN
    This castle hath a pleasant seat. The air
    Nimbly and sweetly recommends itself
    Unto our gentle senses.

5. **martlet:** house martin; **approve:** demonstrate

6. **By his loved mansionry:** i.e., by the fact that he loves to build nests here

7. **wooingly:** invitingly; **jutty:** projection

8. **coign of vantage:** i.e., protruding corner **of vantage:** affording a good observation point

9. **pendant:** hanging, suspended; **procreant cradle:** cradle where he breeds

14–15. **The love . . . as love:** i.e., the affection of others who attend on us is sometimes inconvenient, but we are still grateful for it

15–17. **Herein . . . trouble:** i.e., in saying this, I teach you how to say "thank you" for the trouble I'm causing you, since it is the result of my love **God 'ild:** God yield (i.e., thank you)

20. **single:** trivial

20–21. **contend / Against:** rival, try to match

22. **those:** i.e., those honors

23. **late:** recent

24. **We rest your hermits:** we remain your beadsmen (Beadsmen repaid gifts with prayers for the donor. See picture, page 114.)

26. **We:** i.e., I (royal plural); **coursed:** pursued

27. **purveyor:** a servant who makes advance preparations for a noble master

33. **theirs:** i.e., their dependents; **what is theirs:** what they own; **in compt:** in trust (from the king)

35. **Still:** always

BANQUO   This guest of summer,
  The temple-haunting ⌜martlet,⌝ does approve,   5
  By his loved ⌜mansionry,⌝ that the heaven's breath
  Smells wooingly here. No jutty, frieze,
  Buttress, nor coign of vantage, but this bird
  Hath made his pendant bed and procreant cradle.
  Where they ⌜most⌝ breed and haunt, I have   10
    observed,
  The air is delicate.

Enter Lady ⌜Macbeth.⌝

DUNCAN   See, see our honored hostess!—
  The love that follows us sometime is our trouble,
  Which still we thank as love. Herein I teach you   15
  How you shall bid God 'ild us for your pains
  And thank us for your trouble.
LADY MACBETH   All our service,
  In every point twice done and then done double,
  Were poor and single business to contend   20
  Against those honors deep and broad wherewith
  Your Majesty loads our house. For those of old,
  And the late dignities heaped up to them,
  We rest your hermits.
DUNCAN   Where's the Thane of Cawdor?   25
  We coursed him at the heels and had a purpose
  To be his purveyor; but he rides well,
  And his great love (sharp as his spur) hath helped
    him
  To his home before us. Fair and noble hostess,   30
  We are your guest tonight.
LADY MACBETH   Your servants ever
  Have theirs, themselves, and what is theirs in compt
  To make their audit at your Highness' pleasure,
  Still to return your own.   35
DUNCAN   Give me your hand.

1.7 Macbeth contemplates the reasons why it is a terrible thing to kill Duncan. Lady Macbeth mocks his fears and offers a plan for Duncan's murder, which Macbeth accepts.

---

  0 SD. **Sewer:** butler

  1–2. **If . . . quickly:** This sentence plays with several meanings of **done** (finished with, accomplished, performed) and for the moment leaves **it** unspecified.

  3. **trammel up:** catch as in a net

  4. **his surcease:** Duncan's death; or its (the assassination's) completion; **that but:** if only

  7. **jump the life to come:** risk the fate of my soul

  17. **Hath . . . meek:** has exercised his power so humbly (or so compassionately)

  18. **clear:** blameless

  19. **plead . . . against:** as in a court of law

  20. **taking-off:** i.e., murder

  22. **Striding the blast:** riding the wind; **cherubin:**

(continued)

A trammel net. (1.7.3)
From *Fables d'Esope* (1678).

⌈*Taking her hand.*⌉
Conduct me to mine host. We love him highly
And shall continue our graces towards him.
By your leave, hostess.

They exit.

Scene 7
*Hautboys. Torches. Enter a Sewer and divers Servants
with dishes and service over the stage. Then enter
Macbeth.*

MACBETH
If it were done when 'tis done, then 'twere well
It were done quickly. If th' assassination
Could trammel up the consequence and catch
With his surcease success, that but this blow
Might be the be-all and the end-all here,   5
But here, upon this bank and ⌈shoal⌉ of time,
We'd jump the life to come. But in these cases
We still have judgment here, that we but teach
Bloody instructions, which, being taught, return
To plague th' inventor. This even-handed justice   10
Commends th' ingredience of our poisoned chalice
To our own lips. He's here in double trust:
First, as I am his kinsman and his subject,
Strong both against the deed; then, as his host,
Who should against his murderer shut the door,   15
Not bear the knife myself. Besides, this Duncan
Hath borne his faculties so meek, hath been
So clear in his great office, that his virtues
Will plead like angels, trumpet-tongued, against
The deep damnation of his taking-off;   20
And pity, like a naked newborn babe
Striding the blast, or heaven's cherubin horsed

In other plays, Shakespeare uses the word **cherubin** to refer to cherubs (winged angels, depicted as infants or youths with wings and rosy, smiling faces); here, the reference seems to be to the powerful supernatural winged creature described in Ezekiel 10 and referred to in Psalm 18.10, where God comes to the rescue of the psalmist, David, riding on a cherub (". . . he rode upon a Cherub and did fly, and he came flying upon the wings of the wind").

23. **sightless couriers:** invisible coursers or steeds

25. **That:** so that; **tears shall drown the wind:** i.e., tears as thick as rain will still the wind

27. **which o'erleaps itself:** i.e., the rider, in vaulting into the saddle, jumps too far and falls on the other side

35. **bought:** acquired

37. **would be:** ought to be, wish to be

41. **green and pale:** sickly, as if hung over from drinking

43. **Such:** i.e., fickle, like his hope and resolution

48. **wait upon:** always follow, accompany

49. **the poor cat i' th' adage:** i.e., the cat who would eat fish but would not get its feet wet (proverbial)   **adage:** proverb

52. **none:** i.e., not a man

Upon the sightless couriers of the air,
Shall blow the horrid deed in every eye,
That tears shall drown the wind. I have no spur   25
To prick the sides of my intent, but only
Vaulting ambition, which o'erleaps itself
And falls on th' other—

Enter Lady ⌜Macbeth.⌝

How now, what news?
LADY MACBETH
He has almost supped. Why have you left the   30
    chamber?
MACBETH
Hath he asked for me?
LADY MACBETH   Know you not he has?
MACBETH
We will proceed no further in this business.
He hath honored me of late, and I have bought   35
Golden opinions from all sorts of people,
Which would be worn now in their newest gloss,
Not cast aside so soon.
LADY MACBETH   Was the hope drunk
Wherein you dressed yourself? Hath it slept since?   40
And wakes it now, to look so green and pale
At what it did so freely? From this time
Such I account thy love. Art thou afeard
To be the same in thine own act and valor
As thou art in desire? Wouldst thou have that   45
Which thou esteem'st the ornament of life
And live a coward in thine own esteem,
Letting "I dare not" wait upon "I would,"
Like the poor cat i' th' adage?
MACBETH   Prithee, peace.   50
I dare do all that may become a man.
Who dares ⌜do⌝ more is none.

55. **break:** broach, disclose
56. **durst:** dared
58. **Nor . . . nor:** neither . . . nor
59. **adhere:** agree, conjoin
60. **that their fitness:** their very convenience (for the assassination)
62. **unmake:** i.e., unman, unnerve
70. **But:** only; **screw . . . place:** i.e., screw up your courage (Perhaps the image is that of a crossbow string that is mechanically tightened into its notch.)
72. **Whereto the rather:** to which all the sooner
73. **Soundly invite him:** i.e., invite him to sleep soundly; **chamberlains:** servants of the bedchamber
74. **wassail:** carousing; **convince:** overpower (Latin *vincere*, to conquer)
75. **warder:** guardian
76. **receipt of reason:** container that encloses reason
77. **limbeck:** alembic (the upper part of a still into which fumes rise)
78. **drenchèd natures:** drowned faculties
80. **put upon:** impute to, blame on
81. **spongy:** i.e., having soaked up wine
82. **quell:** murder
84. **mettle:** spirit; metal
85. **received:** accepted as true

A crossbow. (1.7.70)
From Wilhelm Dilich, *Krieges-Schule* (1689).

LADY MACBETH   What beast was 't,
   then,
  That made you break this enterprise to me?   55
  When you durst do it, then you were a man;
  And to be more than what you were, you would
  Be so much more the man. Nor time nor place
  Did then adhere, and yet you would make both.
  They have made themselves, and that their fitness   60
   now
  Does unmake you. I have given suck, and know
  How tender 'tis to love the babe that milks me.
  I would, while it was smiling in my face,
  Have plucked my nipple from his boneless gums   65
  And dashed the brains out, had I so sworn as you
  Have done to this.
MACBETH   If we should fail—
LADY MACBETH   We fail?
  But screw your courage to the sticking place   70
  And we'll not fail. When Duncan is asleep
  (Whereto the rather shall his day's hard journey
  Soundly invite him), his two chamberlains
  Will I with wine and wassail so convince
  That memory, the warder of the brain,   75
  Shall be a fume, and the receipt of reason
  A limbeck only. When in swinish sleep
  Their drenchèd natures lies as in a death,
  What cannot you and I perform upon
  Th' unguarded Duncan? What not put upon   80
  His spongy officers, who shall bear the guilt
  Of our great quell?
MACBETH   Bring forth men-children only,
  For thy undaunted mettle should compose
  Nothing but males. Will it not be received,   85
  When we have marked with blood those sleepy two
  Of his own chamber and used their very daggers,
  That they have done 't?

89. **other:** otherwise
92. **settled:** determined
92–93. **bend . . . agent:** exert all the power in my body
93. **to:** i.e., to perform
94. **mock:** deceive

LADY MACBETH   Who dares receive it other,
  As we shall make our griefs and clamor roar   90
  Upon his death?
MACBETH   I am settled and bend up
  Each corporal agent to this terrible feat.
  Away, and mock the time with fairest show.
  False face must hide what the false heart doth   95
    know.

They exit.

The Tragedy of

MACBETH

ACT 2

2.1 Banquo, who has accompanied Duncan to Inverness, is uneasy because he too is tempted by the witches' prophecies, although only in his dreams. Macbeth pretends to have forgotten them. Left alone by Banquo, Macbeth imagines that he sees a gory dagger leading him to Duncan's room. Hearing the bell rung by Lady Macbeth to signal completion of her preparations for Duncan's death, Macbeth exits to kill the king.

---

6. **husbandry:** careful use of resources, frugality
7. **Take thee that:** perhaps giving Fleance his dagger
8. **heavy summons:** summons to sleep
17. **largess:** gifts, tips; **offices:** i.e., servants

Tarquin and Lucrece. (2.1.67)
From Jost Amman, *Icones Livianae* (1572).

ACT 2

Scene 1

Enter Banquo, and Fleance with a torch before him.

BANQUO   How goes the night, boy?

FLEANCE
The moon is down. I have not heard the clock.

BANQUO   And she goes down at twelve.

FLEANCE   I take 't 'tis later, sir.

BANQUO
Hold, take my sword.   ⌜*Giving his sword to Fleance.*⌝   5
                      There's husbandry in heaven;
Their candles are all out. Take thee that too.
A heavy summons lies like lead upon me,
And yet I would not sleep. Merciful powers,
Restrain in me the cursèd thoughts that nature   10
Gives way to in repose.

     Enter Macbeth, and a Servant with a torch.

                    Give me my sword.—Who's
  there?

MACBETH   A friend.

BANQUO
What, sir, not yet at rest? The King's abed.   15
He hath been in unusual pleasure, and
Sent forth great largess to your offices.
This diamond he greets your wife withal,

49

19. **shut up:** concluded (his remarks); or summed up (what he had to say)

22–23. **Our will . . . wrought:** our desire (to entertain the king properly) was limited (by our lack of time to prepare); otherwise our desire would have operated freely, liberally **will:** desire **became the servant to defect:** was subjected to deficiency **wrought:** operated

29. **entreat an hour to serve:** i.e., find a time that suits us

34. **cleave to my consent:** i.e., support me, join my party **cleave:** adhere

37. **still:** always, continue to

38. **My bosom franchised:** my inmost being free

39. **I shall be counseled:** I will be willing to listen; or, I will follow your counsel

48. **fatal vision:** an apparition (1) that is ominous or fateful, (2) that represents a deadly weapon, or (3) that shows what is fated, sent by Fate

48–49. **sensible / To feeling:** perceptible to the sense of touch

By the name of most kind hostess, and shut up
In measureless content.   20
                    ⌜*He gives Macbeth a diamond.*⌝
MACBETH   Being unprepared,
  Our will became the servant to defect,
  Which else should free have wrought.
BANQUO   All's well.
  I dreamt last night of the three Weïrd Sisters.   25
  To you they have showed some truth.
MACBETH   I think not of
    them.
  Yet, when we can entreat an hour to serve,
  We would spend it in some words upon that   30
    business,
  If you would grant the time.
BANQUO   At your kind'st leisure.
MACBETH
  If you shall cleave to my consent, when 'tis,
  It shall make honor for you.   35
BANQUO   So I lose none
  In seeking to augment it, but still keep
  My bosom franchised and allegiance clear,
  I shall be counseled.
MACBETH   Good repose the while.   40
BANQUO   Thanks, sir. The like to you.
                    Banquo ⌜*and Fleance*⌝ *exit.*
MACBETH
  Go bid thy mistress, when my drink is ready,
  She strike upon the bell. Get thee to bed.
                              ⌜*Servant*⌝ *exits.*
  Is this a dagger which I see before me,
  The handle toward my hand? Come, let me clutch   45
    thee.
  I have thee not, and yet I see thee still.
  Art thou not, fatal vision, sensible
  To feeling as to sight? Or art thou but

50. **false:** unreal

51. **heat-oppressèd:** feverishly excited

54. **marshal'st:** lead

56. **made the fools o' th' other senses:** made fools of by the evidence given by my sense of touch

57. **Or else worth all the rest:** or else my eyes alone report the truth

58. **dudgeon:** handle; **gouts:** clots

59. **There's no such thing:** i.e., the dagger does not exist

62. **abuse:** deceive

64. **Hecate:** goddess of witchcraft (**pale** because of the connection with the moon); **off'rings:** sacrifices, rituals

65. **Alarumed:** summoned to action (*all' arme*, to arms!)

66. **watch:** i.e., cry, like that of a watchman; **thus:** Macbeth here begins to move with the stealthy pace of a murderer, toward his design.

67. **Tarquin:** a Roman infamous for his rape of Lucrece (Shakespeare had told the story of the rape and Lucrece's suicide in his *The Rape of Lucrece* [1594].); **ravishing:** ravenous; leading to rape

72. **take ... time:** take away (with the sound of his footsteps) the horror of the moment's absolute silence

73. **suits:** agrees, fits in

74. **Words ... gives:** i.e., talking simply cools off the heat that drives action

A dagger of the mind, a false creation   50
Proceeding from the heat-oppressèd brain?
I see thee yet, in form as palpable
As this which now I draw.   ⌜*He draws his dagger.*⌝
Thou marshal'st me the way that I was going,
And such an instrument I was to use.   55
Mine eyes are made the fools o' th' other senses
Or else worth all the rest. I see thee still,
And, on thy blade and dudgeon, gouts of blood,
Which was not so before. There's no such thing.
It is the bloody business which informs   60
Thus to mine eyes. Now o'er the one-half world
Nature seems dead, and wicked dreams abuse
The curtained sleep. Witchcraft celebrates
Pale Hecate's off'rings, and withered murder,
Alarumed by his sentinel, the wolf,   65
Whose howl's his watch, thus with his stealthy pace,
With Tarquin's ravishing ⌜strides,⌝ towards his
   design
Moves like a ghost. Thou ⌜sure⌝ and firm-set earth,
Hear not my steps, which ⌜way they⌝ walk, for fear   70
Thy very stones prate of my whereabouts
And take the present horror from the time,
Which now suits with it. Whiles I threat, he lives.
Words to the heat of deeds too cold breath gives.
                                        A bell rings.
I go, and it is done. The bell invites me.   75
Hear it not, Duncan, for it is a knell
That summons thee to heaven or to hell.
                                        He exits.

2.2 Lady Macbeth waits anxiously for Macbeth to return from killing Duncan. When Macbeth enters, he is horrified by what he has done. He has brought with him the daggers that he used on Duncan, instead of leaving them in the room with Duncan's servants as Lady Macbeth had planned. When he finds himself incapable of returning the daggers, Lady Macbeth does so. She returns to find Macbeth still paralyzed with horror and urges him to put on his gown and wash the blood from his hands.

---

5. **bellman:** town crier, who sounded the hours of the night and tolled the bell on the evening before an execution (Here, the **owl** is a bellman because, according to superstition, the hoot of the owl portends death. He is **fatal** perhaps because sent by Fate, or perhaps because he predicts death.)

6. **He:** Macbeth

8. **mock their charge:** make a mockery of their responsibility

9. **possets:** hot drinks, containing milk and liquor

15. **Confounds:** ruins

16. **He:** Macbeth; **he:** Duncan

Scene 2
Enter Lady ⌜Macbeth.⌝

LADY MACBETH
  That which hath made them drunk hath made me
    bold.
  What hath quenched them hath given me fire.
    Hark!—Peace.
  It was the owl that shrieked, the fatal bellman,   5
  Which gives the stern'st good-night. He is about it.
  The doors are open, and the surfeited grooms
  Do mock their charge with snores. I have drugged
    their possets,
  That death and nature do contend about them   10
  Whether they live or die.
MACBETH, ⌜*within*⌝   Who's there? what, ho!
LADY MACBETH
  Alack, I am afraid they have awaked,
  And 'tis not done. Th' attempt and not the deed
  Confounds us. Hark!—I laid their daggers ready;   15
  He could not miss 'em. Had he not resembled
  My father as he slept, I had done 't.

Enter Macbeth ⌜with bloody daggers.⌝

  My husband?
MACBETH
  I have done the deed. Didst thou not hear a noise?
LADY MACBETH
  I heard the owl scream and the crickets cry.   20
  Did not you speak?
MACBETH   When?
LADY MACBETH   Now.
MACBETH   As I descended?
LADY MACBETH Ay.   25
MACBETH Hark!—Who lies i' th' second chamber?
LADY MACBETH Donalbain.

28. **sorry:** deplorable, wretched
34. **addressed them:** applied themselves
38. **As:** as if; **hangman's:** executioner's (The hangman also had to cut the body to pieces, hence his bloody hands.)
39. **List'ning:** i.e., listening to
46. **so:** if so
49. **raveled sleave:** tangled threads
51. **second course:** i.e., main course

A bellman. (2.2.5)
From Thomas Dekker, *The belman of London* (1616).

MACBETH   This is a sorry sight.

LADY MACBETH
A foolish thought, to say a sorry sight.

MACBETH
There's one did laugh in 's sleep, and one cried   30
   "Murder!"
That they did wake each other. I stood and heard
   them.
But they did say their prayers and addressed them
Again to sleep.   35

LADY MACBETH   There are two lodged together.

MACBETH
One cried "God bless us" and "Amen" the other,
As they had seen me with these hangman's hands,
List'ning their fear. I could not say "Amen"
When they did say "God bless us."   40

LADY MACBETH   Consider it not so deeply.

MACBETH
But wherefore could not I pronounce "Amen"?
I had most need of blessing, and "Amen"
Stuck in my throat.

LADY MACBETH   These deeds must not be thought   45
After these ways; so, it will make us mad.

MACBETH
Methought I heard a voice cry "Sleep no more!
Macbeth does murder sleep"—the innocent sleep,
Sleep that knits up the raveled sleave of care,
The death of each day's life, sore labor's bath,   50
Balm of hurt minds, great nature's second course,
Chief nourisher in life's feast.

LADY MACBETH   What do you mean?

MACBETH
Still it cried "Sleep no more!" to all the house.
"Glamis hath murdered sleep, and therefore   55
   Cawdor
Shall sleep no more. Macbeth shall sleep no more."

59. **unbend:** loosen, slacken (contrasts with "bend up" at 1.7.92)

60. **brainsickly:** madly; or, morbidly

61. **witness:** evidence

72. **gild:** i.e., smear; **withal:** with it (i.e., with Duncan's blood)

80. **multitudinous:** vast; **incarnadine:** turn blood-red

81. **one red:** i.e., a uniform red color

82. **shame:** would be ashamed

87. **constancy:** firmness of mind

88. **left you unattended:** abandoned you

LADY MACBETH
  Who was it that thus cried? Why, worthy thane,
  You do unbend your noble strength to think
  So brainsickly of things. Go get some water   60
  And wash this filthy witness from your hand.—
  Why did you bring these daggers from the place?
  They must lie there. Go, carry them and smear
  The sleepy grooms with blood.

MACBETH   I'll go no more.   65
  I am afraid to think what I have done.
  Look on 't again I dare not.

LADY MACBETH   Infirm of purpose!
  Give me the daggers. The sleeping and the dead
  Are but as pictures. 'Tis the eye of childhood   70
  That fears a painted devil. If he do bleed,
  I'll gild the faces of the grooms withal,
  For it must seem their guilt.
            She exits ⌜with the daggers.⌝ Knock within.

MACBETH   Whence is that
  knocking?   75
  How is 't with me when every noise appalls me?
  What hands are here! Ha, they pluck out mine eyes.
  Will all great Neptune's ocean wash this blood
  Clean from my hand? No, this my hand will rather
  The multitudinous seas incarnadine,   80
  Making the green one red.

Enter Lady ⌜Macbeth.⌝

LADY MACBETH
  My hands are of your color, but I shame
  To wear a heart so white.   *Knock.*
              I hear a knocking
  At the south entry. Retire we to our chamber.   85
  A little water clears us of this deed.
  How easy is it, then! Your constancy
  Hath left you unattended.   *Knock.*

90. **nightgown:** dressing gown; **occasion:** circumstances

91. **show us to be watchers:** reveal that we are still up and awake

92. **poorly:** poor-spiritedly, dispiritedly

2.3 A drunken porter goes to answer a knocking at the gate, all the while playing the role of a devil-porter at the gates of hell. He admits Macduff and Lennox, who have come to wake Duncan. Macbeth appears and greets them. Macduff exits to wake Duncan, then returns to announce Duncan's murder. Macbeth and Lennox go to see for themselves. When they return, Lennox announces that Duncan's servants are the murderers. Macbeth reveals that he has slain the servants. When his motives are questioned, Lady Macbeth interrupts by calling for help for herself. Duncan's sons, Malcolm and Donalbain, plan to flee for their lives, Malcolm to England, Donalbain to Ireland.

---

0 SD. **Porter:** gatekeeper

2. **old:** i.e., plenty of

4. **Beelzebub:** Matthew 12.24: "Beelzebub, the prince of the devils"

4–5. **farmer . . . plenty:** perhaps, the farmer hoarded crops only to face an unexpected surplus and dropping prices

6. **napkins:** handkerchiefs (to mop up his sweat)

8. **equivocator:** one who intentionally speaks ambiguously, either by using words that can be taken

(continued)

      Hark, more knocking.
Get on your nightgown, lest occasion call us   90
And show us to be watchers. Be not lost
So poorly in your thoughts.
MACBETH
To know my deed 'twere best not know myself.
            Knock.
Wake Duncan with thy knocking. I would thou
 couldst.   95
           They exit.

      Scene 3
   Knocking within. Enter a Porter.

PORTER Here's a knocking indeed! If a man were
 porter of hell gate, he should have old turning the
 key. *(Knock.)* Knock, knock, knock! Who's there, i'
 th' name of Beelzebub? Here's a farmer that hanged
 himself on th' expectation of plenty. Come in time! 5
 Have napkins enough about you; here you'll sweat
 for 't. *(Knock.)* Knock, knock! Who's there, in th'
 other devil's name? Faith, here's an equivocator
 that could swear in both the scales against either
 scale, who committed treason enough for God's 10
 sake yet could not equivocate to heaven. O, come in,
 equivocator. *(Knock.)* Knock, knock, knock! Who's
 there? Faith, here's an English tailor come hither for
 stealing out of a French hose. Come in, tailor. Here
 you may roast your goose. *(Knock.)* Knock, knock! 15
 Never at quiet.—What are you?—But this place is
 too cold for hell. I'll devil-porter it no further. I had
 thought to have let in some of all professions that go
 the primrose way to th' everlasting bonfire. *(Knock.)*
 Anon, anon!   20

⌜*The Porter opens the door to*⌝ *Macduff and Lennox.*

 I pray you, remember the porter.

more than one way or by mentally hedging or limiting his or her words (Jesuits were charged with equivocation, and many scholars see this passage as referring to the 1606 trial and execution for treason of a Jesuit, Father Garnett, whose defense included the claim that, by the doctrine of equivocation, a lie is not a lie if the speaker intends a second, true meaning by his words.)

14. **stealing . . . hose:** stealing cloth in the process of making breeches (with perhaps an obscene suggestion)

15. **roast your goose:** heat your tailor's iron ("Goose" was also a slang term for prostitute.)

19. **primrose way . . . bonfire:** the broad and pleasurable path to hell (See Matthew 7.13.)

20. **Anon:** right away

21. **I pray you, remember the porter:** This is a request for a tip.

24–25. **the second cock:** i.e., 3 A.M.

29. **nose-painting:** reddening the nose through drink

37. **giving him the lie:** lying to him; laying him out

40. **i' th' very throat on me:** in my very throat (To "give a lie in the throat" was to accuse someone of deep, deliberate lying.) **on:** of

42. **took up my legs:** lifted my feet off the ground (an image from wrestling), perhaps in a drunken stagger

43. **made a shift:** managed; **cast him:** give him a fall (as in wrestling); throw it out (vomit, urinate)

50. **timely:** early

51. **slipped the hour:** allowed the hour to slip by

MACDUFF
  Was it so late, friend, ere you went to bed
  That you do lie so late?

PORTER Faith, sir, we were carousing till the second
  cock, and drink, sir, is a great provoker of three   25
  things.

MACDUFF What three things does drink especially pro-
  voke?

PORTER Marry, sir, nose-painting, sleep, and urine.
  Lechery, sir, it provokes and unprovokes. It pro-   30
  vokes the desire, but it takes away the performance. Therefore much drink may be said to be an
  equivocator with lechery. It makes him, and it
  mars him; it sets him on, and it takes him off; it
  persuades him and disheartens him; makes him   35
  stand to and not stand to; in conclusion, equivo-
  cates him in a sleep and, giving him the lie, leaves
  him.

MACDUFF I believe drink gave thee the lie last night.

PORTER That it did, sir, i' th' very throat on me; but I   40
  requited him for his lie, and, I think, being too
  strong for him, though he took up my legs sometime, yet I made a shift to cast him.

MACDUFF Is thy master stirring?

Enter Macbeth.

  Our knocking has awaked him. Here he comes.   45
                    ⌜*Porter exits.*⌝

LENNOX
  Good morrow, noble sir.

MACBETH   Good morrow, both.

MACDUFF
  Is the King stirring, worthy thane?

MACBETH   Not yet.

MACDUFF
  He did command me to call timely on him.   50
  I have almost slipped the hour.

55. **physics:** relieves (To "physic" was to treat an illness with physic, or medicine.)

58. **limited service:** appointed duty

60. **appoint:** plan to do

62. **as:** i.e., so

66. **combustion:** tumult, confusion

67. **obscure bird:** bird of darkness, the owl
obscure: accent first syllable

76. **Confusion:** destruction

78. **The Lord's anointed temple:** the body of the king, which was represented by Renaissance monarchies as having been anointed by God

MACBETH   I'll bring you to him.

MACDUFF
I know this is a joyful trouble to you,
But yet 'tis one.

MACBETH
The labor we delight in physics pain.   55
This is the door.

MACDUFF   I'll make so bold to call,
For 'tis my limited service.   *Macduff exits.*

LENNOX   Goes the King hence today?

MACBETH   He does. He did appoint so.   60

LENNOX
The night has been unruly. Where we lay,
Our chimneys were blown down and, as they say,
Lamentings heard i' th' air, strange screams of
   death,
And prophesying, with accents terrible,   65
Of dire combustion and confused events
New hatched to th' woeful time. The obscure bird
Clamored the livelong night. Some say the earth
Was feverous and did shake.

MACBETH   'Twas a rough night.   70

LENNOX
My young remembrance cannot parallel
A fellow to it.

Enter Macduff.

MACDUFF   O horror, horror, horror!
Tongue nor heart cannot conceive nor name thee!

MACBETH and LENNOX   What's the matter?   75

MACDUFF
Confusion now hath made his masterpiece.
Most sacrilegious murder hath broke ope
The Lord's anointed temple and stole thence
The life o' th' building.

83. **Gorgon:** a mythological figure whose glance brought instant death

90. **great doom's image:** a sight as terrible as doomsday

91. **As . . . sprites:** as if, at the Last Judgment, you rise from your graves like ghosts

92. **countenance:** be in keeping with

94. **calls to parley:** The image is of the battlefield, where a "parley" is a conference.

98. **repetition:** report, account

Perseus with the Gorgon's head. (2.3.83)
From Cesare Ripa, *Noua iconologia* (1618).

MACBETH   What is 't you say? The life?   80
LENNOX   Mean you his Majesty?
MACDUFF
    Approach the chamber and destroy your sight
    With a new Gorgon. Do not bid me speak.
    See and then speak yourselves.
                        Macbeth and Lennox exit.
                            Awake, awake!   85
    Ring the alarum bell.—Murder and treason!
    Banquo and Donalbain, Malcolm, awake!
    Shake off this downy sleep, death's counterfeit,
    And look on death itself. Up, up, and see
    The great doom's image. Malcolm, Banquo,   90
    As from your graves rise up and walk like sprites
    To countenance this horror.—Ring the bell.
                                Bell rings.

                Enter Lady ⌜Macbeth.⌝

LADY MACBETH   What's the business,
    That such a hideous trumpet calls to parley
    The sleepers of the house? Speak, speak!   95
MACDUFF   O gentle lady,
    'Tis not for you to hear what I can speak.
    The repetition in a woman's ear
    Would murder as it fell.

                Enter Banquo.

                    O Banquo, Banquo,   100
    Our royal master's murdered.
LADY MACBETH   Woe, alas!
    What, in our house?
BANQUO   Too cruel anywhere.—
    Dear Duff, I prithee, contradict thyself   105
    And say it is not so.

107. **but:** only; **chance:** occurrence

109. **nothing serious in mortality:** nothing important in life

110. **toys:** trifles; **grace:** honor

111–12. **The wine . . . brag of:** i.e., the **vault** has had the wine drawn off and nothing is left but the dregs (**lees**)

113–14. **What is amiss? / You are:** i.e., "What is wrong?" "You are damaged (**amiss**) in that your father is killed."

115. **head:** fountainhead, source

120. **badged:** marked, as with badges

122. **distracted:** distraught

127. **amazed:** utterly confused, bewildered

128. **in a moment:** simultaneously

129. **expedition:** haste

132. **breach:** gap (technically, a break in a fortification caused by battering)

133. **wasteful:** destructive

Enter Macbeth, Lennox, and Ross.

MACBETH
  Had I but died an hour before this chance,
  I had lived a blessèd time; for from this instant
  There's nothing serious in mortality.
  All is but toys. Renown and grace is dead.   110
  The wine of life is drawn, and the mere lees
  Is left this vault to brag of.

Enter Malcolm and Donalbain.

DONALBAIN   What is amiss?
MACBETH   You are, and do not know 't.
  The spring, the head, the fountain of your blood   115
  Is stopped; the very source of it is stopped.
MACDUFF
  Your royal father's murdered.
MALCOLM   O, by whom?
LENNOX
  Those of his chamber, as it seemed, had done 't.
  Their hands and faces were all badged with blood.   120
  So were their daggers, which unwiped we found
  Upon their pillows. They stared and were distracted.
  No man's life was to be trusted with them.
MACBETH
  O, yet I do repent me of my fury,
  That I did kill them.   125
MACDUFF   Wherefore did you so?
MACBETH
  Who can be wise, amazed, temp'rate, and furious,
  Loyal, and neutral, in a moment? No man.
  Th' expedition of my violent love
  Outrun the pauser, reason. Here lay Duncan,   130
  His silver skin laced with his golden blood,
  And his gashed stabs looked like a breach in nature
  For ruin's wasteful entrance; there the murderers,

134. **Steeped:** soaked

135. **Unmannerly breeched with gore:** i.e., improperly clothed with blood (instead of being properly sheathed); **refrain:** hold himself back

137. **make 's:** make his

138. **Help me hence, ho!:** Lady Macbeth perhaps faints—or pretends to faint—at this point.

142. **That . . . ours:** i.e., that have the best right to speak on this subject

144. **Hid in an auger hole:** concealed in a tiny crack (i.e., hiding in ambush)

146. **upon the foot of motion:** ready to move, to take action

148. **naked frailties hid:** i.e., clothed our frail bodies

150. **question:** examine

151. **scruples:** suspicions

153. **undivulged pretense:** unrevealed purpose (of the traitor)

157. **briefly:** quickly; **put on manly readiness:** clothe ourselves properly (with perhaps also a sense of emotional readiness)

160. **consort:** join in league

161. **office:** function

Steeped in the colors of their trade, their daggers
Unmannerly breeched with gore. Who could refrain   135
That had a heart to love, and in that heart
Courage to make 's love known?
LADY MACBETH   Help me hence, ho!
MACDUFF
    Look to the lady.
MALCOLM, ⌜*aside to Donalbain*⌝ Why do we hold our   140
        tongues,
    That most may claim this argument for ours?
DONALBAIN, ⌜*aside to Malcolm*⌝
    What should be spoken here, where our fate,
    Hid in an auger hole, may rush and seize us?
    Let's away. Our tears are not yet brewed.   145
MALCOLM, ⌜*aside to Donalbain*⌝
    Nor our strong sorrow upon the foot of motion.
BANQUO   Look to the lady.
                    ⌜*Lady Macbeth is assisted to leave.*⌝
    And when we have our naked frailties hid,
    That suffer in exposure, let us meet
    And question this most bloody piece of work   150
    To know it further. Fears and scruples shake us.
    In the great hand of God I stand, and thence
    Against the undivulged pretense I fight
    Of treasonous malice.
MACDUFF   And so do I.   155
ALL   So all.
MACBETH
    Let's briefly put on manly readiness
    And meet i' th' hall together.
ALL   Well contented.
                    ⌜*All but Malcolm and Donalbain*⌝ exit.
MALCOLM
    What will you do? Let's not consort with them.   160
    To show an unfelt sorrow is an office
    Which the false man does easy. I'll to England.

165–66. **The near . . . bloody:** a common expression, reminiscent of Matthew 10.36: "a man's foes shall be they of his own household" **near:** nearer

170. **dainty of:** polite about

171. **shift away:** go away stealthily

2.4 An old man and Ross exchange accounts of recent unnatural happenings. Macduff joins them to report that Malcolm and Donalbain are now accused of having bribed the servants who supposedly killed Duncan. Macduff also announces that Macbeth has been chosen king. Ross leaves for Scone and Macbeth's coronation, but Macduff resolves to stay at his own castle at Fife.

---

1. **Threescore and ten:** seventy years

3. **sore:** dreadful

5. **trifled former knowings:** made my earlier experiences seem trivial

8. **his bloody stage:** i.e., the earth, on which man performs his bloody acts

10–12. **Is 't night's . . . kiss it?:** i.e., is it dark because night has become more powerful than day, or because day is hiding its face in shame?

15. **tow'ring in her pride of place:** circling at the top of her ascent

16. **by a mousing owl hawked at:** attacked on the wing by an owl, whose normal prey is mice

DONALBAIN
  To Ireland I. Our separated fortune
  Shall keep us both the safer. Where we are,
  There's daggers in men's smiles. The near in blood,   165
  The nearer bloody.
MALCOLM   This murderous shaft that's shot
  Hath not yet lighted, and our safest way
  Is to avoid the aim. Therefore to horse,
  And let us not be dainty of leave-taking   170
  But shift away. There's warrant in that theft
  Which steals itself when there's no mercy left.

                                   They exit.

Scene 4
Enter Ross with an Old Man.

OLD MAN
  Threescore and ten I can remember well,
  Within the volume of which time I have seen
  Hours dreadful and things strange, but this sore
    night
  Hath trifled former knowings.   5
ROSS   Ha, good father,
  Thou seest the heavens, as troubled with man's act,
  Threatens his bloody stage. By th' clock 'tis day,
  And yet dark night strangles the traveling lamp.
  Is 't night's predominance or the day's shame   10
  That darkness does the face of earth entomb
  When living light should kiss it?
OLD MAN   'Tis unnatural,
  Even like the deed that's done. On Tuesday last
  A falcon, tow'ring in her pride of place,   15
  Was by a mousing owl hawked at and killed.
ROSS
  And Duncan's horses (a thing most strange and
    certain),

19. **minions of their race:** choicest examples of their breed

21. **as:** as if

23. **eat:** ate

34. **good:** i.e., benefit (for themselves); **pretend:** intend

35. **suborned:** secretly bribed

40. **Thriftless:** unprofitable; **ravin up:** devour hungrily

43. **Scone:** the ancient royal city where Scottish kings were crowned

44. **invested:** dressed in his coronation robes; crowned

46. **Colmekill:** the small island (now called Iona), off the coast of Scotland, where Scottish kings were buried

47. **storehouse:** i.e., crypt, where the bodies were placed

Beauteous and swift, the minions of their race,
Turned wild in nature, broke their stalls, flung out,   20
Contending 'gainst obedience, as they would
Make war with mankind.
OLD MAN   'Tis said they eat each
    other.
ROSS
They did so, to th' amazement of mine eyes   25
That looked upon 't.

                Enter Macduff.

                    Here comes the good
    Macduff.—
How goes the world, sir, now?
MACDUFF   Why, see you not?   30
ROSS
Is 't known who did this more than bloody deed?
MACDUFF
Those that Macbeth hath slain.
ROSS   Alas the day,
    What good could they pretend?
MACDUFF   They were suborned.   35
    Malcolm and Donalbain, the King's two sons,
    Are stol'n away and fled, which puts upon them
    Suspicion of the deed.
ROSS   'Gainst nature still!
    Thriftless ambition, that will ravin up   40
    Thine own lives' means. Then 'tis most like
    The sovereignty will fall upon Macbeth.
MACDUFF
    He is already named and gone to Scone
    To be invested.
ROSS   Where is Duncan's body?   45
MACDUFF   Carried to Colmekill,
    The sacred storehouse of his predecessors
    And guardian of their bones.

50. **Fife:** Macduff's castle
51. **thither:** i.e., to Scone
55. **benison:** blessing

Coronation of a Scottish king. (2.4.43–44)
From Raphael Holinshed, *The historie of Scotland* (1577).

ROSS   Will you to Scone?
MACDUFF
  No, cousin, I'll to Fife.   50
ROSS   Well, I will thither.
MACDUFF
  Well, may you see things well done there. Adieu,
  Lest our old robes sit easier than our new.
ROSS   Farewell, father.
OLD MAN
  God's benison go with you and with those   55
  That would make good of bad and friends of foes.

                                All exit.

The Tragedy of

MACBETH

ACT 3

3.1 Banquo suspects that Macbeth killed Duncan in order to become king. Macbeth invites Banquo to a feast that night. Banquo promises to return in time. Macbeth, fearing that Banquo's children, not his own, will be the future kings of Scotland, seizes upon the opportunity provided by Banquo's scheduled return after dark to arrange for his murder. To carry out the crime, Macbeth employs two men whom he has persuaded to regard Banquo as an enemy.

---

4. **stand:** remain

8. **by:** judging by; **on thee made good:** made good with regard to you

10 SD. **Sennet:** flourish of trumpets to announce the entrance of a person of high degree

13. **It had:** it would have; **as:** like

14. **all-thing:** wholly

15. **solemn:** ceremonial

ACT 3

Scene 1
Enter Banquo.

BANQUO
  Thou hast it now—King, Cawdor, Glamis, all
  As the Weïrd Women promised, and I fear
  Thou played'st most foully for 't. Yet it was said
  It should not stand in thy posterity,
  But that myself should be the root and father   5
  Of many kings. If there come truth from them
  (As upon thee, Macbeth, their speeches shine)
  Why, by the verities on thee made good,
  May they not be my oracles as well,
  And set me up in hope? But hush, no more.   10

  Sennet sounded. Enter Macbeth as King, Lady
  ⌈*Macbeth,*⌉ *Lennox, Ross, Lords, and Attendants.*

MACBETH
  Here's our chief guest.
LADY MACBETH   If he had been forgotten,
  It had been as a gap in our great feast
  And all-thing unbecoming.
MACBETH
  Tonight we hold a solemn supper, sir,   15
  And I'll request your presence.
BANQUO
                                Let your Highness

81

18. **Command upon me:** i.e., royally invite me (as opposed to **request,** line 16); **the which:** i.e., your commands; **duties:** obligations

29–30. **I . . . twain:** i.e., I must ride an hour or two after dark

33. **cousins:** Malcolm and Donalbain

36. **invention:** fictions

37. **therewithal:** in addition to that; **cause of state:** state affairs

38. **Craving us jointly:** requiring the attention of both of us; **Hie:** hurry

45. **society:** (your) companionship

46. **The sweeter welcome:** the more sweetly welcome (to me)

46–47. **we will . . . alone:** I will stay . . . alone

47. **While then, God be with you:** until then, good-bye

Command upon me, to the which my duties
Are with a most indissoluble tie
Forever knit.   20
MACBETH   Ride you this afternoon?
BANQUO   Ay, my good lord.
MACBETH
We should have else desired your good advice
(Which still hath been both grave and prosperous)
In this day's council, but we'll take tomorrow.   25
Is 't far you ride?
BANQUO
As far, my lord, as will fill up the time
'Twixt this and supper. Go not my horse the better,
I must become a borrower of the night
For a dark hour or twain.   30
MACBETH   Fail not our feast.
BANQUO   My lord, I will not.
MACBETH
We hear our bloody cousins are bestowed
In England and in Ireland, not confessing
Their cruel parricide, filling their hearers   35
With strange invention. But of that tomorrow,
When therewithal we shall have cause of state
Craving us jointly. Hie you to horse. Adieu,
Till you return at night. Goes Fleance with you?
BANQUO
Ay, my good lord. Our time does call upon 's.   40
MACBETH
I wish your horses swift and sure of foot,
And so I do commend you to their backs.
Farewell.   *Banquo exits.*
Let every man be master of his time
Till seven at night. To make society   45
The sweeter welcome, we will keep ourself
Till suppertime alone. While then, God be with you.
        Lords ⌜and all but Macbeth and a Servant⌝ exit.

48. **Sirrah:** term of address to a social inferior

48–49. **Attend . . . pleasure:** i.e., are those men waiting to see me?

50. **without:** outside

55. **would be:** ought to be

57. **to:** in addition to

61. **genius:** attendant spirit; **rebuked:** checked

62. **Caesar:** i.e., Octavius Caesar (Shakespeare will write about this again in *Antony and Cleopatra.*)

66. **fruitless:** without offspring

70. **issue:** descendants; **filed:** made foul, defiled

72. **rancors:** bitter ill-feelings

73. **eternal jewel:** i.e., soul

74. **common enemy:** i.e., the devil **common:** general

75. **seeds:** sons

76. **come fate:** let fate come; **list:** lists, arena for trial by combat

77. **champion me:** oppose me; **to th' utterance:** to the death (*à l'outrance,* to the uttermost, to extremity)

77 SD. **Murderers:** Although the two men are called "murderers" in the Folio stage directions and speech prefixes, Macbeth's speeches to them suggest that the men are not yet murderers, but are rather very poor men who are desperate and who can thus be persuaded to kill for the king. The thrust of Macbeth's speeches to them is, first, that Banquo is the one responsible for their extreme poverty and, second, that Macbeth will reward them handsomely for the killing. The secondary meanings of such terms as **crossed** and **instruments** (lines 88, 89) suggest that the men have been **beggared** (line 101) by being dispossessed of their property by a greedy

(continued)

Sirrah, a word with you. Attend those men
Our pleasure?
SERVANT
They are, my lord, without the palace gate.   50
MACBETH
Bring them before us.   *Servant exits.*
                         To be thus is nothing,
But to be safely thus. Our fears in Banquo
Stick deep, and in his royalty of nature
Reigns that which would be feared. 'Tis much he   55
   dares,
And to that dauntless temper of his mind
He hath a wisdom that doth guide his valor
To act in safety. There is none but he
Whose being I do fear; and under him   60
My genius is rebuked, as it is said
Mark Antony's was by Caesar. He chid the sisters
When first they put the name of king upon me
And bade them speak to him. Then, prophet-like,
They hailed him father to a line of kings.   65
Upon my head they placed a fruitless crown
And put a barren scepter in my grip,
Thence to be wrenched with an unlineal hand,
No son of mine succeeding. If 't be so,
For Banquo's issue have I filed my mind;   70
For them the gracious Duncan have I murdered,
Put rancors in the vessel of my peace
Only for them, and mine eternal jewel
Given to the common enemy of man
To make them kings, the seeds of Banquo kings.   75
Rather than so, come fate into the list,
And champion me to th' utterance.—Who's there?

         Enter Servant and two Murderers.

⌜*To the Servant.*⌝ Now go to the door, and stay there
   till we call.   *Servant exits.*

landowner (a process described in many writings of the time); they are now **reckless what [they] do** (lines 123–24), willing to undertake anything that will **mend** their lives (line 128).

87. **in probation:** in proving it

88. **borne in hand:** deceived, deluded (from the French *maintenir*); **crossed:** thwarted; also barred, debarred, shut out

89. **instruments:** means; also legal instruments such as were often used to strip men of their property

92. **To half a soul:** i.e., even to a half-wit; **a notion:** an understanding, a mind

98. **gospeled:** ruled by the Gospel's "love your enemies"

101. **yours:** your descendants

103. **catalogue:** list (of human types); **go for:** i.e., are counted as

106. **Shoughs:** rough-haired lap dogs; **water-rugs:** perhaps, water spaniels; **demi-wolves:** crossbreeds of dog and wolf   **demi:** half; **clept:** called

107. **valued file:** a list that evaluates each breed

109. **housekeeper:** watch dog

111. **closed:** enclosed

Was it not yesterday we spoke together? 80
⌈MURDERERS⌉
  It was, so please your Highness.
MACBETH   Well then, now
  Have you considered of my speeches? Know
  That it was he, in the times past, which held you
  So under fortune, which you thought had been 85
  Our innocent self. This I made good to you
  In our last conference, passed in probation with you
  How you were borne in hand, how crossed, the
    instruments,
  Who wrought with them, and all things else that 90
    might
  To half a soul and to a notion crazed
  Say "Thus did Banquo."
FIRST MURDERER   You made it known to us.
MACBETH
  I did so, and went further, which is now 95
  Our point of second meeting. Do you find
  Your patience so predominant in your nature
  That you can let this go? Are you so gospeled
  To pray for this good man and for his issue,
  Whose heavy hand hath bowed you to the grave 100
  And beggared yours forever?
FIRST MURDERER   We are men, my liege.
MACBETH
  Ay, in the catalogue you go for men,
  As hounds and greyhounds, mongrels, spaniels,
    curs, 105
  Shoughs, water-rugs, and demi-wolves are clept
  All by the name of dogs. The valued file
  Distinguishes the swift, the slow, the subtle,
  The housekeeper, the hunter, every one
  According to the gift which bounteous nature 110
  Hath in him closed; whereby he does receive

112. **Particular addition:** a special name or title

112–13. **from the bill . . . alike:** in distinction from the catalogue that simply lists them all as *dogs*

119. **in his life:** because Banquo is alive

120. **were perfect:** would be completely contented

126. **tugged with:** pulled about by

127. **set:** stake, venture; **chance:** eventuality

128. **on 't:** of it

132. **in such bloody distance:** in such mortal hostility; or, within such a **distance** (a technical term in fencing) that I am made bloody (the image continues with the term **thrusts,** line 133)

134. **my near'st of life:** i.e., the part most essential to life—the heart; my most vital spot

136. **bid my will avouch it:** offer my desire for Banquo's death as sufficient justification for killing him

137. **For:** because of

138. **but wail:** i.e., but I must, instead, bewail

140. **to . . . make love:** court your help

Particular addition, from the bill
That writes them all alike. And so of men.
Now, if you have a station in the file,
Not i' th' worst rank of manhood, say 't,   115
And I will put that business in your bosoms
Whose execution takes your enemy off,
Grapples you to the heart and love of us,
Who wear our health but sickly in his life,
Which in his death were perfect.   120
SECOND MURDERER   I am one, my liege,
Whom the vile blows and buffets of the world
Hath so incensed that I am reckless what
I do to spite the world.
FIRST MURDERER   And I another   125
So weary with disasters, tugged with fortune,
That I would set my life on any chance,
To mend it or be rid on 't.
MACBETH   Both of you
Know Banquo was your enemy.   130
⌐MURDERERS⌐   True, my lord.
MACBETH
So is he mine, and in such bloody distance
That every minute of his being thrusts
Against my near'st of life. And though I could
With barefaced power sweep him from my sight   135
And bid my will avouch it, yet I must not,
For certain friends that are both his and mine,
Whose loves I may not drop, but wail his fall
Who I myself struck down. And thence it is
That I to your assistance do make love,   140
Masking the business from the common eye
For sundry weighty reasons.
SECOND MURDERER   We shall, my lord,
Perform what you command us.
FIRST MURDERER   Though our lives—   145

146. **spirits:** courage, vital powers

149. **perfect spy o' th' time:** perhaps, exact information about when the deed should be done

150. **on 't:** of it

151. **something from:** somewhat away from; **always thought:** it being always understood

152. **I require a clearness:** I must be kept clear

153. **rubs nor botches:** flaws or defects

155. **material:** important

157. **Resolve yourselves apart:** make up your minds in private

160. **straight:** straightway, immediately

161. **concluded:** decided

3.2 Both Lady Macbeth and Macbeth express their unhappiness. Macbeth speaks of his fear of Banquo especially. He refers to a dreadful deed that will happen that night but does not confide his plan for Banquo's murder to Lady Macbeth.

_____

6. **spent:** used up, exhausted

MACBETH
Your spirits shine through you. Within this hour at
    most
I will advise you where to plant yourselves,
Acquaint you with the perfect spy o' th' time,
The moment on 't, for 't must be done tonight   150
And something from the palace; always thought
That I require a clearness. And with him
(To leave no rubs nor botches in the work)
Fleance, his son, that keeps him company,
Whose absence is no less material to me   155
Than is his father's, must embrace the fate
Of that dark hour. Resolve yourselves apart.
I'll come to you anon.
⌜MURDERERS⌝ We are resolved, my lord.
MACBETH
I'll call upon you straight. Abide within.   160
                                    ⌜*Murderers exit.*⌝
It is concluded. Banquo, thy soul's flight,
If it find heaven, must find it out tonight.
                                    ⌜*He exits.*⌝

Scene 2
Enter Macbeth's Lady and a Servant.

LADY MACBETH   Is Banquo gone from court?
SERVANT
Ay, madam, but returns again tonight.
LADY MACBETH
Say to the King I would attend his leisure
For a few words.
SERVANT Madam, I will.   *He exits.*   5
LADY MACBETH   Naught's had, all's spent,
Where our desire is got without content.
'Tis safer to be that which we destroy
Than by destruction dwell in doubtful joy.

11. **sorriest:** most wretched

13. **without:** beyond

15. **scorched:** slashed (from *score,* to slash as with a knife)

16. **close:** come back together, heal; **our poor malice:** your and my weak hostility

17. **her former tooth:** i.e., the snake's tooth (her poisoned fang) as it was before she was **scorched**

18. **frame:** structure; **disjoint:** come apart

18-19. **both the worlds suffer:** (let) heaven and ⸢th perish

25. **In restless ecstasy:** in a frenzy of sleeplessness

27. **his:** its; **nor . . . nor:** neither . . . nor

28. **Malice domestic:** civil ill will; **foreign levy:** armies from abroad

30. **gentle my lord:** my noble lord

31. **Sleek o'er:** smooth over; **rugged looks:** i.e., furrowed brows

35-36. **present . . . tongue:** give him special honor by look and speech

36. **unsafe the while that:** (you and I) are unsafe during this time in which

37. **lave our honors:** wash our reputations

38. **vizards:** masks, visors

40. **leave this:** stop talking and thinking this way

Enter Macbeth.

How now, my lord, why do you keep alone,   10
Of sorriest fancies your companions making,
Using those thoughts which should indeed have died
With them they think on? Things without all remedy
Should be without regard. What's done is done.

MACBETH
We have scorched the snake, not killed it.   15
She'll close and be herself whilst our poor malice
Remains in danger of her former tooth.
But let the frame of things disjoint, both the worlds
 suffer,
Ere we will eat our meal in fear, and sleep   20
In the affliction of these terrible dreams
That shake us nightly. Better be with the dead,
Whom we, to gain our peace, have sent to peace,
Than on the torture of the mind to lie
In restless ecstasy. Duncan is in his grave.   25
After life's fitful fever he sleeps well.
Treason has done his worst; nor steel nor poison,
Malice domestic, foreign levy, nothing
Can touch him further.

LADY MACBETH   Come on, gentle my lord,   30
Sleek o'er your rugged looks. Be bright and jovial
Among your guests tonight.

MACBETH   So shall I, love,
And so I pray be you. Let your remembrance
Apply to Banquo; present him eminence   35
Both with eye and tongue: unsafe the while that we
Must lave our honors in these flattering streams
And make our faces vizards to our hearts,
Disguising what they are.

LADY MACBETH   You must leave this.   40

MACBETH
O, full of scorpions is my mind, dear wife!
Thou know'st that Banquo and his Fleance lives.

43. **nature's copy's not eterne:** i.e., they have not been granted eternal life **copy:** perhaps, copyhold tenure (a lease held by the lord of the manor); or, the individual copied from nature's mold

46. **cloistered:** secluded (in the dark buildings and belfries where the bat flies); **Hecate:** a powerful goddess and the patron of witches

47. **shard-borne:** borne on wings that are like shards (pieces of pottery)

48. **rung night's yawning peal:** i.e., finished announcing, with its **hums,** the coming of sleepy night (The image is of the pealing of the curfew bell.)

52. **seeling night:** i.e., night which blinds the eyes (The image is of the sewing together of the eyelids of the falcon to keep it temporarily in darkness.)

53. **Scarf up:** blindfold; **pitiful:** compassionate

57. **rooky:** perhaps, filled with rooks

3.3 A third man joins the two whom Macbeth has already sent to kill Banquo and Fleance. The three assassins manage to kill Banquo. Fleance escapes.

---

3. **He:** i.e., the third murderer; **delivers:** reports

4. **offices:** duties

5. **To the direction just:** exactly according to (our) instructions (from Macbeth)

LADY MACBETH
  But in them nature's copy's not eterne.
MACBETH
  There's comfort yet; they are assailable.
  Then be thou jocund. Ere the bat hath flown   45
  His cloistered flight, ere to black Hecate's summons
  The shard-borne beetle with his drowsy hums
  Hath rung night's yawning peal, there shall be done
  A deed of dreadful note.
LADY MACBETH   What's to be done?   50
MACBETH
  Be innocent of the knowledge, dearest chuck,
  Till thou applaud the deed.—Come, seeling night,
  Scarf up the tender eye of pitiful day
  And with thy bloody and invisible hand
  Cancel and tear to pieces that great bond   55
  Which keeps me pale. Light thickens, and the crow
  Makes wing to th' rooky wood.
  Good things of day begin to droop and drowse,
  Whiles night's black agents to their preys do
    rouse.—   60
  Thou marvel'st at my words, but hold thee still.
  Things bad begun make strong themselves by ill.
  So prithee go with me.
                                          They exit.

                        Scene 3
                Enter three Murderers.

FIRST MURDERER
  But who did bid thee join with us?
THIRD MURDERER   Macbeth.
SECOND MURDERER, ⌈*to the First Murderer*⌉
  He needs not our mistrust, since he delivers
  Our offices and what we have to do
  To the direction just.   5

8. **lated:** belated, tardy

9. **timely:** opportune, welcome

10. **The subject of our watch:** the person we are waiting for

14. **within the note of expectation:** i.e., included in the list of expected guests

16. **His horses go about:** perhaps, the horses are being led or ridden on a more circuitous route

A Scottish thane killed in ambush. (3.3.24–26)
From Raphael Holinshed, *The historie of Scotland* (1577).

FIRST MURDERER   Then stand with us.—
The west yet glimmers with some streaks of day.
Now spurs the lated traveler apace
To gain the timely inn, ⌜and⌝ near approaches
The subject of our watch.   10
THIRD MURDERER Hark, I hear horses.
BANQUO, *within* Give us a light there, ho!
SECOND MURDERER Then 'tis he. The rest
That are within the note of expectation
Already are i' th' court.   15
FIRST MURDERER His horses go about.
THIRD MURDERER
Almost a mile; but he does usually
(So all men do) from hence to th' palace gate
Make it their walk.

           Enter Banquo and Fleance, with a torch.

SECOND MURDERER A light, a light!   20
THIRD MURDERER 'Tis he.
FIRST MURDERER Stand to 't.
BANQUO It will be rain tonight.
FIRST MURDERER Let it come down!
                   ⌜*The three Murderers attack.*⌝
BANQUO
O treachery! Fly, good Fleance, fly, fly, fly!   25
Thou mayst revenge—O slave!
                   ⌜*He dies. Fleance exits.*⌝
THIRD MURDERER
Who did strike out the light?
FIRST MURDERER   Was 't not the way?
THIRD MURDERER There's but one down. The son is
    fled.   30
SECOND MURDERER We have lost best half of our
    affair.
FIRST MURDERER
Well, let's away and say how much is done.
                            They exit.

3.4   As Macbeth's banquet begins, one of Banquo's murderers appears at the door to tell Macbeth of Banquo's death and Fleance's escape. Returning to the table, Macbeth is confronted by Banquo's ghost, invisible to all but Macbeth. While Lady Macbeth is able to dismiss as a momentary fit Macbeth's expressions of horror at the ghost's first appearance, the reappearance of the ghost and Macbeth's outcries in response to it force Lady Macbeth to send all the guests away. Alone with Lady Macbeth, Macbeth resolves to meet the witches again. He foresees a future marked by further violence.

---

1. **degrees:** relative status (and hence where you are entitled to sit)

1–2. **At first / And last:** to all in whatever degree

6. **keeps her state:** remains on her throne; **in best time:** at the most proper moment

7. **require:** request

10. **encounter thee:** respond to your welcome (perhaps with low bows as they take their places)

11. **Both sides are even:** (1) the thanks of the guests balance the welcome of Lady Macbeth, so the hostess and guests are even; or, (2) there are equal numbers on both sides of the table

12. **large:** liberal, unrestrained; **Anon:** soon; **measure:** i.e., a toast

21. **the nonpareil:** without equal

23. **I . . . perfect:** I would otherwise have been fully secure, complete

Scene 4

*Banquet prepared. Enter Macbeth, Lady ⌐Macbeth,¬
Ross, Lennox, Lords, and Attendants.*

MACBETH
  You know your own degrees; sit down. At first
  And last, the hearty welcome.   ⌐*They sit.*¬
LORDS   Thanks to your Majesty.
MACBETH
  Ourself will mingle with society
  And play the humble host.   5
  Our hostess keeps her state, but in best time
  We will require her welcome.
LADY MACBETH
  Pronounce it for me, sir, to all our friends,
  For my heart speaks they are welcome.

          Enter First Murderer ⌐to the door.¬

MACBETH
  See, they encounter thee with their hearts' thanks.   10
  Both sides are even. Here I'll sit i' th' midst.
  Be large in mirth. Anon we'll drink a measure
  The table round. ⌐*Approaching the Murderer.*¬ There's
    blood upon thy face.
MURDERER   'Tis Banquo's then.   15
MACBETH
  'Tis better thee without than he within.
  Is he dispatched?
MURDERER
  My lord, his throat is cut. That I did for him.
MACBETH
  Thou art the best o' th' cutthroats,
  Yet he's good that did the like for Fleance.   20
  If thou didst it, thou art the nonpareil.
MURDERER
  Most royal sir, Fleance is 'scaped.
MACBETH, ⌐*aside*¬
  Then comes my fit again. I had else been perfect,

24. **founded:** rooted, stable

25. **broad:** free; **casing:** surrounding, enclosing

26. **cabined, cribbed:** closed in, cramped (as in a cabin or hovel)

27. **saucy:** insolent; **safe:** i.e., safely disposed of

28. **bides:** remains; waits

30. **The least a death to nature:** the smallest one of which would have been fatal

32. **worm:** serpent larva (i.e., a creature that will grow up to be a serpent)

35. **hear ourselves:** talk

37. **give the cheer:** i.e., entertain your guests properly; **sold:** i.e., as opposed to **given** (line 39), as if the host were an innkeeper (The sense, lines 37–39, is that a feast is no better than a meal in an inn if the host does not keep assuring his guests of their welcome.)

39. **To feed . . . home:** mere eating is best done at home

40. **From thence:** i.e., (when one is) away from home; **meat:** food; **ceremony:** the practice of courtesy

41 SD. **Enter the Ghost:** The ghost is not observed by Macbeth until line 54. The ghost may, in fact, enter at line 41, unobserved by Macbeth and the other characters onstage. Or it is possible that the entrance is marked at line 41 because the Folio reproduces a stage manager's note to remind the actor playing Banquo to get ready to enter, at around line 47, when "summoned" by Macbeth.

43. **wait on:** serve, and therefore follow upon

(continued)

Whole as the marble, founded as the rock,
As broad and general as the casing air.   25
But now I am cabined, cribbed, confined, bound in
To saucy doubts and fears.—But Banquo's safe?
MURDERER
Ay, my good lord. Safe in a ditch he bides,
With twenty trenchèd gashes on his head,
The least a death to nature.   30
MACBETH   Thanks for that.
There the grown serpent lies. The worm that's fled
Hath nature that in time will venom breed,
No teeth for th' present. Get thee gone. Tomorrow
We'll hear ourselves again.   *Murderer exits.*   35
LADY MACBETH   My royal lord,
You do not give the cheer. The feast is sold
That is not often vouched, while 'tis a-making,
'Tis given with welcome. To feed were best at home;
From thence, the sauce to meat is ceremony;   40
Meeting were bare without it.

Enter the Ghost of Banquo, and sits in Macbeth's place.

MACBETH, ⌈*to Lady Macbeth*⌉ Sweet remembrancer!—
Now, good digestion wait on appetite
And health on both!
LENNOX   May 't please your Highness sit.   45
MACBETH
Here had we now our country's honor roofed,
Were the gracèd person of our Banquo present,
Who may I rather challenge for unkindness
Than pity for mischance.
ROSS   His absence, sir,   50
Lays blame upon his promise. Please 't your
    Highness
To grace us with your royal company?
MACBETH
The table's full.

46. **our country's honor roofed:** i.e., all the nobility of the country under one roof

48–49. **Who . . . mischance:** whom I hope I should blame for unkindly staying away on purpose rather than pity for some accident that has happened to him

51. **Lays . . . promise:** i.e., calls into question his promise (to be here)

57. **moves:** disturbs

66. **upon a thought:** in a moment

67. **note:** pay attention to

68. **passion:** disturbed state

75. **air-drawn:** made of air

76. **flaws and starts:** outbursts

77. **to:** in comparison to; **well become:** be very appropriate for

79. **Authorized by:** vouched for, with a sense also of "authored by" (accent on second syllable); **Shame itself!:** i.e., for shame!

LENNOX Here is a place reserved, sir. 55
MACBETH Where?
LENNOX
  Here, my good lord. What is 't that moves your
    Highness?
MACBETH
  Which of you have done this?
LORDS What, my good lord? 60
MACBETH, ⌜*to the Ghost*⌝
  Thou canst not say I did it. Never shake
  Thy gory locks at me.
ROSS
  Gentlemen, rise. His Highness is not well.
LADY MACBETH
  Sit, worthy friends. My lord is often thus
  And hath been from his youth. Pray you, keep seat. 65
  The fit is momentary; upon a thought
  He will again be well. If much you note him
  You shall offend him and extend his passion.
  Feed and regard him not. ⌜*Drawing Macbeth aside.*⌝
                    Are you a man? 70
MACBETH
  Ay, and a bold one, that dare look on that
  Which might appall the devil.
LADY MACBETH O, proper stuff!
  This is the very painting of your fear.
  This is the air-drawn dagger which you said 75
  Led you to Duncan. O, these flaws and starts,
  Impostors to true fear, would well become
  A woman's story at a winter's fire,
  Authorized by her grandam. Shame itself!
  Why do you make such faces? When all's done, 80
  You look but on a stool.
MACBETH
  Prithee, see there. Behold, look! ⌜*To the Ghost.*⌝ Lo,
  how say you?

85. **charnel houses:** vaults or small buildings for the bones of the dead

86–87. **our monuments . . . kites:** i.e., our only burial vaults (**monuments**) will be the stomachs (**maws**) of birds of prey (**kites**)

92. **humane:** human; also, humane or kindly; **purged the gentle weal:** cleansed the commonwealth of violence and made it gentle

101. **lack you:** miss your company

107 SD. **Enter Ghost:** The ghost is not observed by Macbeth until line 113. See note on 3.4.41 SD.

113. **Avaunt:** begone; **quit:** leave

A charnel house. (3.4.85)
From Richard Day, *A booke of Christian prayers* (1590).

Why, what care I? If thou canst nod, speak too.—
If charnel houses and our graves must send   85
Those that we bury back, our monuments
Shall be the maws of kites.   ⌜*Ghost exits.*⌝
LADY MACBETH   What, quite unmanned in folly?
MACBETH
If I stand here, I saw him.
LADY MACBETH   Fie, for shame!   90
MACBETH
Blood hath been shed ere now, i' th' olden time,
Ere humane statute purged the gentle weal;
Ay, and since too, murders have been performed
Too terrible for the ear. The ⌜time⌝ has been
That, when the brains were out, the man would die,   95
And there an end. But now they rise again
With twenty mortal murders on their crowns
And push us from our stools. This is more strange
Than such a murder is.
LADY MACBETH   My worthy lord,   100
Your noble friends do lack you.
MACBETH   I do forget.—
Do not muse at me, my most worthy friends.
I have a strange infirmity, which is nothing
To those that know me. Come, love and health to   105
   all.
Then I'll sit down.—Give me some wine. Fill full.

Enter Ghost.

I drink to th' general joy o' th' whole table
And to our dear friend Banquo, whom we miss.
Would he were here! To all and him we thirst,   110
And all to all.
LORDS   Our duties, and the pledge.
          ⌜*They raise their drinking cups.*⌝
MACBETH, ⌜*to the Ghost*⌝
Avaunt, and quit my sight! Let the earth hide thee.
Thy bones are marrowless; thy blood is cold;

115. **speculation:** ability to see

119. **a thing of custom:** something customary

123. **Hyrcan:** from Hyrcania, a part of the Roman Empire located at the southern end of the Caspian Sea (In the *Aeneid*, Hyrcania is associated with tigers.)

124. **nerves:** sinews

126. **desert:** (any) uninhabited place

127. **If trembling I inhabit then:** perhaps, if I then tremble; **protest me:** proclaim me

128. **The baby of a girl:** i.e., a baby girl

129. **mock'ry:** illusion (with perhaps the sense, also, of "that which mocks me")

130. **being gone:** i.e., it being gone

134. **admired:** amazing

137–38. **strange . . . owe:** i.e., feel like a stranger to my own nature   **owe:** own

146. **Stand not . . . going:** i.e., don't delay your exit by insisting on leaving in ceremonial rank order

Thou hast no speculation in those eyes   115
Which thou dost glare with.
LADY MACBETH   Think of this, good
    peers,
But as a thing of custom. 'Tis no other;
Only it spoils the pleasure of the time.   120
MACBETH, ⌜*to the Ghost*⌝ What man dare, I dare.
    Approach thou like the rugged Russian bear,
    The armed rhinoceros, or th' Hyrcan tiger;
    Take any shape but that, and my firm nerves
    Shall never tremble. Or be alive again   125
    And dare me to the desert with thy sword.
    If trembling I inhabit then, protest me
    The baby of a girl. Hence, horrible shadow!
    Unreal mock'ry, hence!   ⌜*Ghost exits.*⌝
                          Why so, being gone,   130
    I am a man again.—Pray you sit still.
LADY MACBETH
    You have displaced the mirth, broke the good
        meeting
    With most admired disorder.
MACBETH   Can such things be   135
    And overcome us like a summer's cloud,
    Without our special wonder? You make me strange
    Even to the disposition that I owe,
    When now I think you can behold such sights
    And keep the natural ruby of your cheeks   140
    When mine is blanched with fear.
ROSS   What sights, my
    lord?
LADY MACBETH
    I pray you, speak not. He grows worse and worse.
    Question enrages him. At once, good night.   145
    Stand not upon the order of your going,
    But go at once.
LENNOX   Good night, and better health
    Attend his Majesty.

154. **Augurs:** i.e., auguries, predictions

155. **By maggot pies and choughs:** i.e., by means of magpies and jackdaws

155–56. **brought forth:** revealed

157. **man of blood:** murderer; **What is the night?:** what time of night is it?

164. **fee'd:** paid (to spy)

165. **betimes:** early

169. **no more:** no further

171. **will to hand:** demand to be carried out

172. **scanned:** thought about carefully

173. **season:** seasoning (i.e., that which preserves and gives flavor or zest)

174. **strange and self-abuse:** remarkable self-delusion

175. **initiate fear:** i.e., fear felt by a beginner, an initiate; **wants:** lacks, needs; **hard use:** practice that hardens one; or, vigorous usage

LADY MACBETH   A kind good night to all.   150
   Lords ⌈*and all but Macbeth and Lady Macbeth*⌉ *exit.*
MACBETH
   It will have blood, they say; blood will have blood.
   Stones have been known to move, and trees to
      speak;
   Augurs and understood relations have
   By maggot pies and choughs and rooks brought   155
      forth
   The secret'st man of blood.—What is the night?
LADY MACBETH
   Almost at odds with morning, which is which.
MACBETH
   How say'st thou that Macduff denies his person
   At our great bidding?   160
LADY MACBETH   Did you send to him, sir?
MACBETH
   I hcar it by the way; but I will send.
   There's not a one of them but in his house
   I keep a servant fee'd. I will tomorrow
   (And betimes I will) to the Weïrd Sisters.   165
   More shall they speak, for now I am bent to know
   By the worst means the worst. For mine own good,
   All causes shall give way. I am in blood
   Stepped in so far that, should I wade no more,
   Returning were as tedious as go o'er.   170
   Strange things I have in head, that will to hand,
   Which must be acted ere they may be scanned.
LADY MACBETH
   You lack the season of all natures, sleep.
MACBETH
   Come, we'll to sleep. My strange and self-abuse
   Is the initiate fear that wants hard use.   175
   We are yet but young in deed.
                              They exit.

3.5 The presentation of the witches in this scene differs from their presentation in the rest of the play (except for 4.1.39–43 and 141–48). Most editors and scholars believe that neither this scene nor the passages in 4.1 were written by Shakespeare.

---

2. **beldams:** hags
7. **close:** secret
15. **Acheron:** a river in the underworld, in Greek mythology
24. **profound:** of deep significance
27. **artificial:** deceitful; skilled in artifice
29. **confusion:** destruction

Scene 5

Thunder. Enter the three Witches, meeting Hecate.

FIRST WITCH
 Why, how now, Hecate? You look angerly.
HECATE
 Have I not reason, beldams as you are?
 Saucy and overbold, how did you dare
 To trade and traffic with Macbeth
 In riddles and affairs of death,   5
 And I, the mistress of your charms,
 The close contriver of all harms,
 Was never called to bear my part
 Or show the glory of our art?
 And which is worse, all you have done   10
 Hath been but for a wayward son,
 Spiteful and wrathful, who, as others do,
 Loves for his own ends, not for you.
 But make amends now. Get you gone,
 And at the pit of Acheron   15
 Meet me i' th' morning. Thither he
 Will come to know his destiny.
 Your vessels and your spells provide,
 Your charms and everything beside.
 I am for th' air. This night I'll spend   20
 Unto a dismal and a fatal end.
 Great business must be wrought ere noon.
 Upon the corner of the moon
 There hangs a vap'rous drop profound.
 I'll catch it ere it come to ground,   25
 And that, distilled by magic sleights,
 Shall raise such artificial sprites
 As by the strength of their illusion
 Shall draw him on to his confusion.
 He shall spurn fate, scorn death, and bear 30
 His hopes 'bove wisdom, grace, and fear.

32. **security:** too much self-confidence

35 SD. **Come away:** This song is from Thomas Middleton's play *The Witch* (Act 3, scene 3). The first two lines read "Come away! Come away! / Hecate, Hecate, come away!" Many scholars think that *Macbeth* 3.5, as well as parts of 4.1, were written by Middleton, perhaps for a revival of the play later in James's reign.

3.6 Lennox and an unnamed lord discuss politics in Scotland. Lennox comments sarcastically upon Macbeth's "official" versions of the many recent violent deaths. The nameless lord responds with news of Macduff's flight to England to seek help in overthrowing Macbeth.

1. **but hit your thoughts:** merely agreed with what you were already thinking

2. **interpret farther:** i.e., go on to draw further conclusions

3. **borne:** managed, conducted

5. **of:** by; **marry:** an interjection, here meaning, loosely, "to be sure" or "indeed"

9. **want the thought:** help thinking

11. **fact:** deed, crime

12. **straight:** immediately

13. **delinquents:** offenders

14. **slaves of drink:** i.e., in a drunken stupor; **thralls:** slaves

20. **an 't:** if it

And you all know, security
Is mortals' chiefest enemy.
                                        Music and a song.
Hark! I am called. My little spirit, see,
Sits in a foggy cloud and stays for me. ⌜*Hecate exits.*⌝   35
                    Sing within "Come away, come away," etc.
FIRST WITCH
Come, let's make haste. She'll soon be back again.
                                        They exit.

Scene 6
Enter Lennox and another Lord.

LENNOX
My former speeches have but hit your thoughts,
Which can interpret farther. Only I say
Things have been strangely borne. The gracious
    Duncan
Was pitied of Macbeth; marry, he was dead.   5
And the right valiant Banquo walked too late,
Whom you may say, if 't please you, Fleance killed,
For Fleance fled. Men must not walk too late.
Who cannot want the thought how monstrous
It was for Malcolm and for Donalbain   10
To kill their gracious father? Damnèd fact,
How it did grieve Macbeth! Did he not straight
In pious rage the two delinquents tear
That were the slaves of drink and thralls of sleep?
Was not that nobly done? Ay, and wisely, too,   15
For 'twould have angered any heart alive
To hear the men deny 't. So that I say
He has borne all things well. And I do think
That had he Duncan's sons under his key
(As, an 't please heaven, he shall not) they should   20
    find
What 'twere to kill a father. So should Fleance.

23. **For from broad words:** as a result of plain speaking

28. **son of Duncan:** i.e., Malcolm

29. **holds:** withholds; **due of birth:** birthright

31. **Of:** by; **Edward:** Edward the Confessor, king of England from 1042 to 1066

32–33. **nothing / Takes:** does not detract

33. **his high respect:** the high respect granted Malcolm

34. **upon his aid:** on Malcolm's behalf

37. **ratify:** sanction

40. **free honors:** honors freely given

45. **an absolute . . . I:** i.e., Macduff had answered Macbeth's order to appear with a peremptory "Sir, not I!"

46. **cloudy:** unhappy, gloomy; **turns me:** i.e., turns

48. **clogs:** burdens

50. **him:** i.e., Macduff

52. **unfold:** reveal

54–55. **our . . . accursed:** i.e., our country, suffering under an accursed hand

A hermit. (1.6.24)
From August Casimir Redel, *Apophtegmata symbolica* (n.d.).

But peace. For from broad words, and 'cause he
    failed
His presence at the tyrant's feast, I hear   25
Macduff lives in disgrace. Sir, can you tell
Where he bestows himself?
LORD   The ⌐son⌐ of Duncan
(From whom this tyrant holds the due of birth)
Lives in the English court and is received   30
Of the most pious Edward with such grace
That the malevolence of fortune nothing
Takes from his high respect. Thither Macduff
Is gone to pray the holy king upon his aid
To wake Northumberland and warlike Siward   35
That, by the help of these (with Him above
To ratify the work), we may again
Give to our tables meat, sleep to our nights,
Free from our feasts and banquets bloody knives,
Do faithful homage, and receive free honors,   40
All which we pine for now. And this report
Hath so exasperate ⌐the⌐ King that he
Prepares for some attempt of war.
LENNOX Sent he to Macduff?
LORD
He did, and with an absolute "Sir, not I,"   45
The cloudy messenger turns me his back
And hums, as who should say "You'll rue the time
That clogs me with this answer."
LENNOX   And that well might
Advise him to a caution ⌐t' hold⌐ what distance   50
His wisdom can provide. Some holy angel
Fly to the court of England and unfold
His message ere he come, that a swift blessing
May soon return to this our suffering country
Under a hand accursed.   55
LORD I'll send my prayers with him.
                          They exit.

The Tragedy of

MACBETH

ACT 4

4.1 Macbeth approaches the witches to learn how to make his kingship secure. In response they summon for him three apparitions: an armed head, a bloody child, and finally a child crowned, with a tree in his hand. These apparitions instruct Macbeth to beware Macduff but reassure him that no man born of woman can harm him and that he will not be overthrown until Birnam Wood moves to Dunsinane. Macbeth is greatly reassured, but his confidence in the future is shaken when the witches show him a line of kings all in the image of Banquo. After the witches disappear, Macbeth discovers that Macduff has fled to England and decides to kill Macduff's family immediately.

---

1. **brinded:** brindled, striped
2. **hedge-pig:** hedgehog
3. **Harpier:** perhaps the Third Witch's familiar
6–9. **Toad . . . pot:** i.e., first boil the toad that has sweated venom for thirty-one days under a cold stone **Sweltered:** exuded
12. **Fillet:** slice; **fenny:** i.e., living in a fen or swamp

ACT 4

Scene 1
Thunder. Enter the three Witches.

FIRST WITCH
Thrice the brinded cat hath mewed.
SECOND WITCH
Thrice, and once the hedge-pig whined.
THIRD WITCH
Harpier cries "'Tis time, 'tis time!"
FIRST WITCH
Round about the cauldron go;
In the poisoned entrails throw.   5
Toad, that under cold stone
Days and nights has thirty-one
Sweltered venom sleeping got,
Boil thou first i' th' charmèd pot.
⌐*The Witches circle the cauldron.*¬
ALL
Double, double toil and trouble;   10
Fire burn, and cauldron bubble.
SECOND WITCH
Fillet of a fenny snake
In the cauldron boil and bake.
Eye of newt and toe of frog,
Wool of bat and tongue of dog,   15
Adder's fork and blindworm's sting,

17. **howlet:** owlet, small owl

23. **mummy:** mummified human flesh; **maw and gulf:** voracious belly

24. **ravined:** perhaps, ravenous; or, glutted

30. **birth-strangled:** i.e., killed as soon as born

31. **drab:** whore

32. **thick and slab:** viscous

33. **chaudron:** entrails

37. **baboon's:** accented on first syllable

39–43. **O . . . in:** These lines (and the stage direction preceding them) are thought by most scholars to be by another author. Since the song that the Witches sing, "Black Spirits," is from Middleton's play *The Witch*, the lines may have been written by Middleton.

Lizard's leg and howlet's wing,
For a charm of powerful trouble,
Like a hell-broth boil and bubble.

ALL
Double, double toil and trouble;   20
Fire burn, and cauldron bubble.

THIRD WITCH
Scale of dragon, tooth of wolf,
Witch's mummy, maw and gulf
Of the ravined salt-sea shark,
Root of hemlock digged i' th' dark,   25
Liver of blaspheming Jew,
Gall of goat and slips of yew
Slivered in the moon's eclipse,
Nose of Turk and Tartar's lips,
Finger of birth-strangled babe   30
Ditch-delivered by a drab,
Make the gruel thick and slab.
Add thereto a tiger's chaudron
For th' ingredience of our cauldron.

ALL
Double, double toil and trouble;   35
Fire burn, and cauldron bubble.

SECOND WITCH
Cool it with a baboon's blood.
Then the charm is firm and good.

Enter Hecate ⌐to⌐ *the other three Witches.*

HECATE
O, well done! I commend your pains,
And everyone shall share i' th' gains.   40
And now about the cauldron sing
Like elves and fairies in a ring,
Enchanting all that you put in.
Music and a song: "Black Spirits," etc. ⌐*Hecate exits.*⌐

54. **yeasty:** foamy, frothy

55. **Confound:** destroy; **navigation:** i.e., ships

56. **bladed corn:** wheat not yet fully ripe; **lodged:** beaten down by wind

58. **warders':** watchmen's

59. **slope:** perhaps, bend, or let fall

62. **nature's germens:** the seeds from which everything springs

63. **sicken:** becomes nauseated (at its own destructiveness)

72. **sweaten:** sweated

SECOND WITCH
By the pricking of my thumbs,
Something wicked this way comes.　　　　　　45
Open, locks,
Whoever knocks.

Enter Macbeth.

MACBETH
How now, you secret, black, and midnight hags?
What is 't you do?
ALL　　　　　　　　　A deed without a name.　　50
MACBETH
I conjure you by that which you profess
(Howe'er you come to know it), answer me.
Though you untie the winds and let them fight
Against the churches, though the yeasty waves
Confound and swallow navigation up,　　　　55
Though bladed corn be lodged and trees blown
　　down,
Though castles topple on their warders' heads,
Though palaces and pyramids do slope
Their heads to their foundations, though the　　60
　　treasure
Of nature's ⌜germens⌝ tumble ⌜all together⌝
Even till destruction sicken, answer me
To what I ask you.
FIRST WITCH　　　　　Speak.　　　　　　　65
SECOND WITCH　　　　　　Demand.
THIRD WITCH　　　　　　　　　We'll answer.
FIRST WITCH
Say if th' hadst rather hear it from our mouths
Or from our masters'.
MACBETH　　　　　　Call 'em. Let me see 'em.　　70
FIRST WITCH
Pour in sow's blood that hath eaten
Her nine farrow; grease that's sweaten

76 SD. **Armed Head:** a helmeted head

84. **harped:** sounded, guessed (as in touching the right string on a harp)

95. **take a bond of fate:** bind fate by a contract, get a guarantee from fate (i.e., make doubly sure that Macbeth will not be harmed)

From the murderers' gibbet throw
Into the flame.
ALL   Come high or low;   75
Thyself and office deftly show.

Thunder. First Apparition, an Armed Head.

MACBETH
Tell me, thou unknown power—
FIRST WITCH   He knows thy
    thought.
Hear his speech but say thou naught.   80
FIRST APPARITION
Macbeth! Macbeth! Macbeth! Beware Macduff!
Beware the Thane of Fife! Dismiss me. Enough.
                                        He descends.
MACBETH
Whate'er thou art, for thy good caution, thanks.
Thou hast harped my fear aright. But one word
    more—   85
FIRST WITCH
He will not be commanded. Here's another
More potent than the first.

Thunder. Second Apparition, a Bloody Child.

SECOND APPARITION   Macbeth! Macbeth! Macbeth!—
MACBETH   Had I three ears, I'd hear thee.
SECOND APPARITION
Be bloody, bold, and resolute. Laugh to scorn   90
The power of man, for none of woman born
Shall harm Macbeth.   ⌜*He*⌝ *descends.*
MACBETH
Then live, Macduff; what need I fear of thee?
But yet I'll make assurance double sure
And take a bond of fate. Thou shalt not live,   95
That I may tell pale-hearted fear it lies,
And sleep in spite of thunder.

99. **like the issue of a king:** in the shape of an heir to a throne

100–1. **round / And top:** crown

104. **chafes:** becomes irritated

109. **impress:** conscript, draft, compel into service

110. **his:** its; **bodements:** prophecies

111. **Rebellious dead:** perhaps in reference to Banquo, who rebelled against death by appearing to Macbeth

113. **live the lease of nature:** i.e., live out his natural life

114. **mortal custom:** a normal (customary) death

Thunder. Third Apparition, a Child Crowned, with a tree in his hand.

           What is this
That rises like the issue of a king
And wears upon his baby brow the round   100
And top of sovereignty?
ALL Listen but speak not to 't.
THIRD APPARITION
 Be lion-mettled, proud, and take no care
 Who chafes, who frets, or where conspirers are.
 Macbeth shall never vanquished be until   105
 Great Birnam Wood to high Dunsinane Hill
 Shall come against him.   ⌜*He*⌝ *descends.*
MACBETH   That will never be.
 Who can impress the forest, bid the tree
 Unfix his earthbound root? Sweet bodements, good! 110
 Rebellious dead, rise never till the wood
 Of Birnam rise, and our high-placed Macbeth
 Shall live the lease of nature, pay his breath
 To time and mortal custom. Yet my heart
 Throbs to know one thing. Tell me, if your art 115
 Can tell so much: shall Banquo's issue ever
 Reign in this kingdom?
ALL   Seek to know no more.
MACBETH
 I will be satisfied. Deny me this,
 And an eternal curse fall on you! Let me know! 120
       ⌜*Cauldron sinks.*⌝ *Hautboys.*
 Why sinks that cauldron? And what noise is this?
FIRST WITCH Show.
SECOND WITCH Show.
THIRD WITCH Show.
ALL
 Show his eyes and grieve his heart.   125
 Come like shadows; so depart.

126 SD. **eight kings:** eight kings of Scotland, including James VI (a supposed descendant of Banquo), who in 1603 also became James I of England; **glass:** mirror

129. **other:** i.e., second

131. **Start:** i.e., burst from your sockets

132. **th' crack of doom:** perhaps, the thunder crash of judgment day; or, the blast of the archangel's trumpet announcing judgment day.

136. **twofold:** double (signifying England and Scotland); **treble:** The reference here is probably to King James's title of "King of Great Britain, France, and Ireland," assumed by him in 1604.

138. **blood-boltered:** i.e., having his hair matted with blood

141–48. **Ay . . . pay:** lines regarded by most scholars as written by another author

142. **amazedly:** as in a trance

143. **sprites:** spirits

146. **antic round:** fantastic dance

150. **aye:** forever

151. **without there:** i.e., you who are outside

*A show of eight kings, ⌜the eighth king⌝ with a glass in
his hand, and Banquo last.*

MACBETH
Thou art too like the spirit of Banquo. Down!
Thy crown does sear mine eyeballs. And thy hair,
Thou other gold-bound brow, is like the first.
A third is like the former.—Filthy hags,   130
Why do you show me this?—A fourth? Start, eyes!
What, will the line stretch out to th' crack of doom?
Another yet? A seventh? I'll see no more.
And yet the eighth appears who bears a glass
Which shows me many more, and some I see   135
That twofold balls and treble scepters carry.
Horrible sight! Now I see 'tis true,
For the blood-boltered Banquo smiles upon me
And points at them for his.
                                   ⌜*The Apparitions disappear.*⌝
                              What, is this so?   140
FIRST WITCH
Ay, sir, all this is so. But why
Stands Macbeth thus amazedly?
Come, sisters, cheer we up his sprites
And show the best of our delights.
I'll charm the air to give a sound   145
While you perform your antic round,
That this great king may kindly say
Our duties did his welcome pay.
                Music. The Witches dance and vanish.
MACBETH
Where are they? Gone? Let this pernicious hour
Stand aye accursèd in the calendar!—   150
Come in, without there.

                    Enter Lennox.

LENNOX   What's your Grace's will?

159. **horse:** horses or horsemen

164. **anticipat'st:** prevents, forestalls; **dread:** dreadful

165–66. **The flighty purpose . . . with it:** i.e., purposes are so fleeting that they escape unless accompanied by acts that fulfill them.

167. **firstlings:** firstborn

171. **surprise:** seize suddenly

174. **trace him in his line:** i.e., are his descendants

176. **sights:** hallucinations

MACBETH
  Saw you the Weïrd Sisters?
LENNOX   No, my lord.
MACBETH
  Came they not by you?   155
LENNOX   No, indeed, my lord.
MACBETH
  Infected be the air whereon they ride,
  And damned all those that trust them! I did hear
  The galloping of horse. Who was 't came by?
LENNOX
  'Tis two or three, my lord, that bring you word   160
  Macduff is fled to England.
MACBETH   Fled to England?
LENNOX   Ay, my good lord.
MACBETH, ⌜*aside*⌝
  Time, thou anticipat'st my dread exploits.
  The flighty purpose never is o'ertook   165
  Unless the deed go with it. From this moment
  The very firstlings of my heart shall be
  The firstlings of my hand. And even now,
  To crown my thoughts with acts, be it thought and
      done: 170
  The castle of Macduff I will surprise,
  Seize upon Fife, give to th' edge o' th' sword
  His wife, his babes, and all unfortunate souls
  That trace him in his line. No boasting like a fool;
  This deed I'll do before this purpose cool.   175
  But no more sights!—Where are these gentlemen?
  Come bring me where they are.
                                        They exit.

4.2 Ross visits Lady Macduff and tries to justify to her Macduff's flight to England, a flight that leaves his family defenseless. After Ross leaves, a messenger arrives to warn Lady Macduff to flee. Before she can do so, Macbeth's men attack her and her son.

---

5. **Our fears do make us traitors:** perhaps, (Macduff's) fear, leading to his flight, makes him a traitor (to his family? to his country?)

11. **He wants the natural touch:** he lacks the natural instinct (to protect his children)

13. **Her young ones in her nest:** i.e., when her young are in the nest

17. **coz:** cousin, kinswoman

18. **school:** control; **for:** as for

20. **The fits o' th' season:** the violent disturbances in (Scotland's political) climate

22–23. **we are traitors . . . ourselves:** we are considered traitors while being unaware of our treason

23–24. **hold rumor / From what we fear:** perhaps, believe what our fears dictate; or judge rumors according to what we fear may happen

27. **Shall not be long but:** i.e., the time will not be long before

Scene 2
Enter Macduff's Wife, her Son, and Ross.

LADY MACDUFF
What had he done to make him fly the land?
ROSS
You must have patience, madam.
LADY MACDUFF   He had none.
His flight was madness. When our actions do not,
Our fears do make us traitors.   5
ROSS   You know not
Whether it was his wisdom or his fear.
LADY MACDUFF
Wisdom? To leave his wife, to leave his babes,
His mansion and his titles in a place
From whence himself does fly? He loves us not;   10
He wants the natural touch; for the poor wren
(The most diminutive of birds) will fight,
Her young ones in her nest, against the owl.
All is the fear, and nothing is the love,
As little is the wisdom, where the flight   15
So runs against all reason.
ROSS   My dearest coz,
I pray you school yourself. But for your husband,
He is noble, wise, judicious, and best knows
The fits o' th' season. I dare not speak much   20
   further;
But cruel are the times when we are traitors
And do not know ourselves; when we hold rumor
From what we fear, yet know not what we fear,
But float upon a wild and violent sea   25
Each way and move—I take my leave of you.
Shall not be long but I'll be here again.
Things at the worst will cease or else climb upward
To what they were before.—My pretty cousin,
Blessing upon you.   30

32–33. should . . . discomfort: i.e., if I should stay longer, (my tears) would disgrace me and make you uncomfortable

37. As birds do: See Matthew 6.26: "Behold the fowls of the air; for they sow not, neither do they reap . . . ; yet your heavenly Father feedeth them."

40–41. the net nor lime, / The pitfall nor the gin: traps for catching birds **lime:** birdlime **gin:** snare (literally, "engine")

42–43. Poor birds . . . set for: i.e., people don't set traps for *poor* birds (birds of little worth)

49. wit: intelligence

50. for thee: for a child

54. swears and lies: Lady Macduff defines a traitor as one who swears an oath of loyalty to a sovereign and then breaks it; the oath, then, is a lie. Her son seems to take "swearing and lying" as general use of profanity and failing to tell the truth.

LADY MACDUFF
  Fathered he is, and yet he's fatherless.
ROSS
  I am so much a fool, should I stay longer
  It would be my disgrace and your discomfort.
  I take my leave at once.   *Ross exits.*
LADY MACDUFF Sirrah, your father's dead.   35
  And what will you do now? How will you live?
SON
  As birds do, mother.
LADY MACDUFF   What, with worms and flies?
SON
  With what I get, I mean; and so do they.
LADY MACDUFF
  Poor bird, thou'dst never fear the net nor lime,   40
  The pitfall nor the gin.
SON
  Why should I, mother? Poor birds they are not set
    for.
  My father is not dead, for all your saying.
LADY MACDUFF
  Yes, he is dead. How wilt thou do for a father?   45
SON Nay, how will you do for a husband?
LADY MACDUFF
  Why, I can buy me twenty at any market.
SON Then you'll buy 'em to sell again.
LADY MACDUFF Thou speak'st with all thy wit,
  And yet, i' faith, with wit enough for thee.   50
SON Was my father a traitor, mother?
LADY MACDUFF Ay, that he was.
SON What is a traitor?
LADY MACDUFF Why, one that swears and lies.
SON And be all traitors that do so?   55
LADY MACDUFF Every one that does so is a traitor
    and must be hanged.
SON And must they all be hanged that swear and lie?

72. **in your state of honor I am perfect:** I know you well as a noble lady

73. **doubt:** fear; **nearly:** very soon; very near

74. **homely:** plain

77. **do worse:** i.e., physically abuse you; **fell:** terrible

78. **Which is too nigh:** i.e., such savage cruelty is all too near

LADY MACDUFF   Every one.

SON   Who must hang them? 60

LADY MACDUFF   Why, the honest men.

SON   Then the liars and swearers are fools, for there
are liars and swearers enough to beat the honest
men and hang up them.

LADY MACDUFF   Now God help thee, poor monkey! But 65
how wilt thou do for a father?

SON   If he were dead, you'd weep for him. If you would
not, it were a good sign that I should quickly have a
new father.

LADY MACDUFF   Poor prattler, how thou talk'st! 70

Enter a Messenger.

MESSENGER
Bless you, fair dame. I am not to you known,
Though in your state of honor I am perfect.
I doubt some danger does approach you nearly.
If you will take a homely man's advice,
Be not found here. Hence with your little ones! 75
To fright you thus methinks I am too savage;
To do worse to you were fell cruelty,
Which is too nigh your person. Heaven preserve
    you!
I dare abide no longer.   *Messenger exits.* 80

LADY MACDUFF   Whither should I fly?
I have done no harm. But I remember now
I am in this earthly world, where to do harm
Is often laudable, to do good sometime
Accounted dangerous folly. Why then, alas, 85
Do I put up that womanly defense
To say I have done no harm?

Enter Murderers.

                    What are these faces?

MURDERER   Where is your husband?

4.3   Macduff finds Malcolm at the English court and urges him to attack Macbeth at once. Malcolm suspects that Macduff is Macbeth's agent sent to lure Malcolm to his destruction in Scotland. After Malcolm tests Macduff and finds him sincere, Malcolm reveals that Edward, king of England, has provided a commander (Siward) and ten thousand troops for the invasion of Scotland. Ross then arrives with the news of the slaughter of Macduff's entire household. At first grief-stricken, Macduff follows Malcolm's advice and converts his grief into a desire to avenge himself on Macbeth.

---

4. **mortal:** deadly; **good men:** i.e., strong fighting men

5. **Bestride . . . birthdom:** i.e., fight to protect our prostrated country (The image is that of a soldier straddling a felled comrade and fighting off the comrade's attackers.)

7. **that:** i.e., so that

9. **Like syllable:** the same (or a comparable) sound

12. **the time to friend:** an opportune (friendly) time

14. **sole:** mere

15. **honest:** honorable

LADY MACDUFF
　I hope in no place so unsanctified　　　　　　　　90
　Where such as thou mayst find him.
MURDERER　　　　　　　　　　　　　He's a traitor.
SON
　Thou liest, thou shag-eared villain!
MURDERER　　　　　　　　　　　What, you egg?
　⌜*Stabbing him.*⌝ Young fry of treachery!　　　　95
SON　　　　　　　　　　　　　　He has killed
　me, mother.
　Run away, I pray you.
　⌜*Lady Macduff*⌝ *exits, crying "Murder!"* ⌜*followed by the*
　　　　　　　　Murderers bearing the Son's body.⌝

Scene 3
Enter Malcolm and Macduff.

MALCOLM
　Let us seek out some desolate shade and there
　Weep our sad bosoms empty.
MACDUFF　　　　　　　　　　Let us rather
　Hold fast the mortal sword and, like good men,
　Bestride our ⌜downfall'n⌝ birthdom. Each new morn　5
　New widows howl, new orphans cry, new sorrows
　Strike heaven on the face, that it resounds
　As if it felt with Scotland, and yelled out
　Like syllable of dolor.
MALCOLM　What I believe, I'll wail;　　　　　　　10
　What know, believe; and what I can redress,
　As I shall find the time to friend, I will.
　What you have spoke, it may be so, perchance.
　This tyrant, whose sole name blisters our tongues,
　Was once thought honest. You have loved him well.　15
　He hath not touched you yet. I am young, but
　　something

18. **and wisdom:** i.e., and consider it wisdom

23–24. **recoil / In an imperial charge:** The general sense is "give way under pressure from a king." The image is that of a gun, loaded, or charged, with powder and shot, recoiling upon itself.

26. **That . . . transpose:** i.e., my thoughts (no matter how negative) cannot change you into something different from what you are

27. **the brightest:** i.e., Lucifer, brightest of the angels, cast from heaven for rebelling against God

28–30. **Though . . . so:** i.e., even though foul things wear, when they can, the look of those in a state of grace, those really in a state of grace nevertheless continue to look gracious

32. **even there:** in the very place

33. **rawness:** vulnerability, unprotectedness

34. **motives:** incitements (to his protective instinct); arguments (for his protection)

36–37. **Let . . . safeties:** i.e., don't assume that my suspicions cast doubts on your honor, but see them as measures taken for my own safety **jealousies:** suspicions

37. **rightly just:** perfectly honorable

40. **basis:** foundations; **sure:** securely, safely

41. **check:** restrain, reprove, curb

41–42. **Wear thou thy wrongs:** i.e., carry (as an heraldic device on your shield) that which you have won through your crimes

43. **The title is affeered:** i.e., Macbeth's title to the crown is confirmed (**affeered**)

48. **absolute fear:** complete mistrust

51. **withal:** as well, at the same time

You may ⌈deserve⌉ of him through me, and wisdom
To offer up a weak, poor, innocent lamb
T' appease an angry god.   20
MACDUFF
I am not treacherous.
MALCOLM   But Macbeth is.
A good and virtuous nature may recoil
In an imperial charge. But I shall crave your
    pardon.   25
That which you are, my thoughts cannot transpose.
Angels are bright still, though the brightest fell.
Though all things foul would wear the brows of
    grace,
Yet grace must still look so.   30
MACDUFF   I have lost my hopes.
MALCOLM
Perchance even there where I did find my doubts.
Why in that rawness left you wife and child,
Those precious motives, those strong knots of love,
Without leave-taking? I pray you,   35
Let not my jealousies be your dishonors,
But mine own safeties. You may be rightly just,
Whatever I shall think.
MACDUFF   Bleed, bleed, poor country!
Great tyranny, lay thou thy basis sure,   40
For goodness dare not check thee. Wear thou thy
    wrongs;
The title is affeered.—Fare thee well, lord.
I would not be the villain that thou think'st
For the whole space that's in the tyrant's grasp,   45
And the rich East to boot.
MALCOLM   Be not offended.
I speak not as in absolute fear of you.
I think our country sinks beneath the yoke.
It weeps, it bleeds, and each new day a gash   50
Is added to her wounds. I think withal

53. **gracious England:** the gracious king of England

58. **More suffer:** shall suffer more

59. **succeed:** i.e., succeed to the throne

62. **particulars:** various kinds; **grafted:** implanted, engrafted

63. **opened:** exposed; or, unfolded like a flower

66. **confineless:** unbounded

71. **Luxurious:** lecherous

72. **Sudden:** violent, without warning

77. **continent:** chaste; also, restraining

78. **will:** lust, carnal appetite

83. **yet:** nevertheless

85. **Convey . . . plenty:** secretly conduct your pleasures on a large scale   **spacious:** ample

86. **cold:** chaste; or, indifferent

There would be hands uplifted in my right;
And here from gracious England have I offer
Of goodly thousands. But, for all this,
When I shall tread upon the tyrant's head   55
Or wear it on my sword, yet my poor country
Shall have more vices than it had before,
More suffer, and more sundry ways than ever,
By him that shall succeed.

MACDUFF   What should he be?   60

MALCOLM
It is myself I mean, in whom I know
All the particulars of vice so grafted
That, when they shall be opened, black Macbeth
Will seem as pure as snow, and the poor state
Esteem him as a lamb, being compared   65
With my confineless harms.

MACDUFF   Not in the legions
Of horrid hell can come a devil more damned
In evils to top Macbeth.

MALCOLM   I grant him bloody,   70
Luxurious, avaricious, false, deceitful,
Sudden, malicious, smacking of every sin
That has a name. But there's no bottom, none,
In my voluptuousness. Your wives, your daughters,
Your matrons, and your maids could not fill up   75
The cistern of my lust, and my desire
All continent impediments would o'erbear
That did oppose my will. Better Macbeth
Than such an one to reign.

MACDUFF   Boundless intemperance   80
In nature is a tyranny. It hath been
Th' untimely emptying of the happy throne
And fall of many kings. But fear not yet
To take upon you what is yours. You may
Convey your pleasures in a spacious plenty   85
And yet seem cold—the time you may so hoodwink.

92. **affection:** disposition

93. **stanchless:** insatiable

95. **his jewels:** the jewels of one subject

102. **summer-seeming:** i.e., summer-beseeming, suitable for the summer of one's youth; or, summer-like and therefore of short duration

103. **The sword . . . kings:** i.e., the cause of the death of our slain kings

104. **foisons:** plentiful supplies

105. **Of your mere own:** from your royal property alone; **portable:** bearable, supportable

106. **With . . . weighed:** balanced against other qualities that are virtuous

108. **As:** such as

109. **lowliness:** humility

111. **relish of:** taste for; trace of

112. **division:** variation, modulation (as if each crime were a piece of music to be played); **several:** distinct

115. **confound:** destroy

We have willing dames enough. There cannot be
That vulture in you to devour so many
As will to greatness dedicate themselves,
Finding it so inclined.   90
MALCOLM   With this there grows
In my most ill-composed affection such
A stanchless avarice that, were I king,
I should cut off the nobles for their lands,
Desire his jewels, and this other's house;   95
And my more-having would be as a sauce
To make me hunger more, that I should forge
Quarrels unjust against the good and loyal,
Destroying them for wealth.
MACDUFF   This avarice   100
Sticks deeper, grows with more pernicious root
Than summer-seeming lust, and it hath been
The sword of our slain kings. Yet do not fear.
Scotland hath foisons to fill up your will
Of your mere own. All these are portable,   105
With other graces weighed.
MALCOLM
But I have none. The king-becoming graces,
As justice, verity, temp'rance, stableness,
Bounty, perseverance, mercy, lowliness,
Devotion, patience, courage, fortitude,   110
I have no relish of them but abound
In the division of each several crime,
Acting it many ways. Nay, had I power, I should
Pour the sweet milk of concord into hell,
Uproar the universal peace, confound   115
All unity on earth.
MACDUFF   O Scotland, Scotland!
MALCOLM
If such a one be fit to govern, speak.
I am as I have spoken.
MACDUFF   Fit to govern?   120

122. **untitled:** i.e., unentitled, usurping

124. **truest issue of thy throne:** heir with the most right to the throne

125. **interdiction:** i.e., censure

126. **blaspheme his breed:** defame his family line (through his scandalous behavior)

129. **Died . . . lived:** died to the world (mortified her flesh through penances and religious exercises) every day of her life

133. **passion:** display of feelings

137. **trains:** wiles, stratagems (such as Macduff's visit seemed to be); **win:** capture, seize

138. **modest wisdom:** wise moderation, prudent caution; **plucks me:** pulls me back

142. **mine own detraction:** my detraction of myself

144. **For:** as

145. **Unknown to woman:** i.e., am a virgin (rather than the lascivious beast that I presented myself as being); **never was forsworn:** have never deliberately broken my oath

150. **upon:** about

153. **warlike:** equipped for battle

154. **at a point:** in readiness

155–156. **we'll . . . quarrel:** i.e., we will travel together (to join Siward), and may our chance of success be as good as our cause is just **goodness:** success **warranted:** justified **quarrel:** ground for action

No, not to live.—O nation miserable,
With an untitled tyrant bloody-sceptered,
When shalt thou see thy wholesome days again,
Since that the truest issue of thy throne
By his own interdiction stands ⌜accursed⌝   125
And does blaspheme his breed?—Thy royal father
Was a most sainted king. The queen that bore thee,
Oft'ner upon her knees than on her feet,
Died every day she lived. Fare thee well.
These evils thou repeat'st upon thyself   130
Hath banished me from Scotland.—O my breast,
Thy hope ends here!
MALCOLM   Macduff, this noble passion,
Child of integrity, hath from my soul
Wiped the black scruples, reconciled my thoughts   135
To thy good truth and honor. Devilish Macbeth
By many of these trains hath sought to win me
Into his power, and modest wisdom plucks me
From overcredulous haste. But God above
Deal between thee and me, for even now   140
I put myself to thy direction and
Unspeak mine own detraction, here abjure
The taints and blames I laid upon myself
For strangers to my nature. I am yet
Unknown to woman, never was forsworn,   145
Scarcely have coveted what was mine own,
At no time broke my faith, would not betray
The devil to his fellow, and delight
No less in truth than life. My first false speaking
Was this upon myself. What I am truly   150
Is thine and my poor country's to command—
Whither indeed, before ⌜thy here-approach,⌝
Old Siward with ten thousand warlike men,
Already at a point, was setting forth.
Now we'll together, and the chance of goodness   155
Be like our warranted quarrel. Why are you silent?

159. **forth:** i.e., out of his private rooms

162. **stay:** await

162–63. **convinces . . . art:** conquers (defeats) the efforts of (medical) science

165. **presently:** immediately

168. **the evil:** i.e., scrofula, or "the king's evil," so-called because the king was thought to have the power to heal it with his touch

172. **strangely visited:** i.e., afflicted by this strange disease

174. **mere:** total, utter

175. **stamp:** a coin stamped with a particular impression

177–78. **To the succeeding royalty . . . benediction:** i.e., to the royal line that will succeed him he bequeaths the power of giving this curative blessing

178. **virtue:** power

MACDUFF
Such welcome and unwelcome things at once
'Tis hard to reconcile.

Enter a Doctor.

MALCOLM
Well, more anon.—Comes the King forth,
I pray you?   160
DOCTOR
Ay, sir. There are a crew of wretched souls
That stay his cure. Their malady convinces
The great assay of art, but at his touch
(Such sanctity hath heaven given his hand)
They presently amend.   165
MALCOLM   I thank you, doctor.
                                          ⌜*Doctor*⌝ *exits.*

MACDUFF
What's the disease he means?
MALCOLM   'Tis called the evil:
A most miraculous work in this good king,
Which often since my here-remain in England   170
I have seen him do. How he solicits heaven
Himself best knows, but strangely visited people
All swoll'n and ulcerous, pitiful to the eye,
The mere despair of surgery, he cures,
Hanging a golden stamp about their necks,   175
Put on with holy prayers; and, 'tis spoken,
To the succeeding royalty he leaves
The healing benediction. With this strange virtue,
He hath a heavenly gift of prophecy,
And sundry blessings hang about his throne   180
That speak him full of grace.

Enter Ross.

MACDUFF   See who comes here.
MALCOLM
My countryman, but yet I know him ⌜not.⌝

185. **betimes:** soon

192. **But who:** except someone who; **once:** ever

193. **rent:** rend, tear

194. **made, not marked:** i.e., so common as to not be noted

195. **modern:** ordinary, commonplace; **ecstasy:** frenzy

198. **or ere they:** before they ever

199. **relation:** report; **nice:** precisely spelled out

200. **grief:** wrong, injury

201. **doth hiss the speaker:** i.e., earns the teller of the injury only hisses because it is already an old story

202. **teems:** brings forth

204. **well:** When spoken of the dead, "well" meant "at peace." The proverb ran: "He is well since he is in Heaven." See *Antony and Cleopatra* 2.5: "we use to say, the dead are well"; *Romeo and Juliet* 5.1: "she is well . . . / Her body sleeps in Capels' monument."

209. **niggard:** miser

MACDUFF
My ever-gentle cousin, welcome hither.

MALCOLM
I know him now.—Good God betimes remove   185
The means that makes us strangers!

ROSS   Sir, amen.

MACDUFF
Stands Scotland where it did?

ROSS   Alas, poor country,
Almost afraid to know itself. It cannot   190
Be called our mother, but our grave, where nothing
But who knows nothing is once seen to smile;
Where sighs and groans and shrieks that rent the air
Are made, not marked; where violent sorrow seems
A modern ecstasy. The dead man's knell   195
Is there scarce asked for who, and good men's lives
Expire before the flowers in their caps,
Dying or ere they sicken.

MACDUFF
O relation too nice and yet too true!

MALCOLM   What's the newest grief?   200

ROSS
That of an hour's age doth hiss the speaker.
Each minute teems a new one.

MACDUFF   How does my wife?

ROSS   Why, well.

MACDUFF   And all my children?   205

ROSS   Well too.

MACDUFF
The tyrant has not battered at their peace?

ROSS
No, they were well at peace when I did leave 'em.

MACDUFF
Be not a niggard of your speech. How goes 't?

ROSS
When I came hither to transport the tidings   210

212. **out:** i.e., in arms, in rebellion

213–14. **witnessed the rather / For that:** confirmed the more readily because

214. **power:** forces; **afoot:** mobilized

215. **of:** for; **Your eye:** i.e., Malcolm's person

217. **doff:** put off, get rid of

221–22. **An older . . . gives out:** i.e., there is no one in the Christian world reputed to be a more experienced or better soldier   **none:** there is none **gives out:** proclaims

225. **would:** ought to

226. **latch:** catch the sound of

229–30. **a fee-grief / Due to some single breast:** a grief belonging to one particular person   **fee-grief:** a term modeled on the term "fee-simple," an estate belonging to one man and his heirs forever   **Due to:** belonging to

240. **surprised:** captured without warning

242. **quarry:** heap

Which I have heavily borne, there ran a rumor
Of many worthy fellows that were out;
Which was to my belief witnessed the rather
For that I saw the tyrant's power afoot.
Now is the time of help. Your eye in Scotland   215
Would create soldiers, make our women fight
To doff their dire distresses.
MALCOLM   Be 't their comfort
We are coming thither. Gracious England hath
Lent us good Siward and ten thousand men;   220
An older and a better soldier none
That Christendom gives out.
ROSS   Would I could answer
This comfort with the like. But I have words
That would be howled out in the desert air,   225
Where hearing should not latch them.
MACDUFF   What concern
   they—
The general cause, or is it a fee-grief
Due to some single breast?   230
ROSS   No mind that's honest
But in it shares some woe, though the main part
Pertains to you alone.
MACDUFF   If it be mine,
Keep it not from me. Quickly let me have it.   235
ROSS
Let not your ears despise my tongue forever,
Which shall possess them with the heaviest sound
That ever yet they heard.
MACDUFF   Hum! I guess at it.
ROSS
Your castle is surprised, your wife and babes   240
Savagely slaughtered. To relate the manner
Were on the quarry of these murdered deer
To add the death of you.
MALCOLM   Merciful heaven!

245. **pull . . . brows:** a conventional gesture of deep sorrow

246–47. **The grief . . . break:** proverb: "grief pent up will break the heart" **Whispers:** whispers to **o'erfraught:** overburdened

250. **from thence:** away from there

255. **He has no children:** Usually taken to mean that Macbeth's lack of children explains his unspeakable cruelty, the words could mean that *Malcolm*'s lack of children explains his rather callous attempts to cheer up Macduff.

256. **hell-kite:** evil bird of prey

259. **Dispute:** fight against

265. **Naught that I am:** i.e., wicked man that I am

270. **play . . . eyes:** i.e., weep

272. **intermission:** delay; **Front to front:** i.e., face to face

What, man, ne'er pull your hat upon your brows.   245
Give sorrow words. The grief that does not speak
Whispers the o'erfraught heart and bids it break.
MACDUFF My children too?
ROSS
Wife, children, servants, all that could be found.
MACDUFF
And I must be from thence? My wife killed too?   250
ROSS I have said.
MALCOLM Be comforted.
Let's make us med'cines of our great revenge
To cure this deadly grief.
MACDUFF
He has no children. All my pretty ones?   255
Did you say "all"? O hell-kite! All?
What, all my pretty chickens and their dam
At one fell swoop?
MALCOLM Dispute it like a man.
MACDUFF I shall do so,   260
But I must also feel it as a man.
I cannot but remember such things were
That were most precious to me. Did heaven look on
And would not take their part? Sinful Macduff,
They were all struck for thee! Naught that I am,   265
Not for their own demerits, but for mine,
Fell slaughter on their souls. Heaven rest them now.
MALCOLM
Be this the whetstone of your sword. Let grief
Convert to anger. Blunt not the heart; enrage it.
MACDUFF
O, I could play the woman with mine eyes   270
And braggart with my tongue! But, gentle heavens,
Cut short all intermission! Front to front
Bring thou this fiend of Scotland and myself.
Within my sword's length set him. If he 'scape,
Heaven forgive him too.   275

278. **Our . . . leave:** we lack nothing now except to take leave (of the king)

280. **Put on:** perhaps, take upon themselves; **instruments:** perhaps, instruments of war

MALCOLM   This ⌜tune⌝ goes manly.
 Come, go we to the King. Our power is ready;
 Our lack is nothing but our leave. Macbeth
 Is ripe for shaking, and the powers above
 Put on their instruments. Receive what cheer you   280
  may.
 The night is long that never finds the day.

They exit.

The Tragedy of

MACBETH

ACT 5

5.1 A gentlewoman who waits on Lady Macbeth has seen her walking in her sleep and has asked a doctor's advice. Together they observe Lady Macbeth make the gestures of repeatedly washing her hands as she relives the horrors that she and Macbeth have carried out and experienced. The doctor concludes that she needs spiritual aid rather than a physician.

---

0 SD. **Physic:** medicine

1. **watched:** stayed awake

3. **walked:** i.e., walked in her sleep

5–6. **nightgown:** dressing gown

6. **closet:** cabinet

11–12. **do the effects of watching:** perform the actions of (someone) awake

17. **meet:** proper

21. **very guise:** usual behavior

22. **close:** hidden

ACT 5

Scene 1

Enter a Doctor of Physic and a Waiting-Gentlewoman.

DOCTOR   I have two nights watched with you but can perceive no truth in your report. When was it she last walked?

GENTLEWOMAN   Since his Majesty went into the field, I have seen her rise from her bed, throw her night-gown upon her, unlock her closet, take forth paper, fold it, write upon 't, read it, afterwards seal it, and again return to bed; yet all this while in a most fast sleep. 5

DOCTOR   A great perturbation in nature, to receive at once the benefit of sleep and do the effects of watching. In this slumb'ry agitation, besides her walking and other actual performances, what at any time have you heard her say? 10

GENTLEWOMAN   That, sir, which I will not report after her. 15

DOCTOR   You may to me, and 'tis most meet you should.

GENTLEWOMAN   Neither to you nor anyone, having no witness to confirm my speech. 20

Enter Lady ⌜Macbeth⌝ with a taper.

Lo you, here she comes. This is her very guise and, upon my life, fast asleep. Observe her; stand close.

161

30. **accustomed:** customary, usual

37. **One. Two.:** She is presumably remembering the clock striking 2 A.M. just before the murder.

43. **mark:** hear, notice

46. **mar all:** upset everything

47. **this starting:** these starts (i.e., sudden fits)

48. **Go to:** for shame

56–57. **sorely charged:** gravely burdened

59. **dignity:** worth

DOCTOR   How came she by that light?

GENTLEWOMAN   Why, it stood by her. She has light by
her continually. 'Tis her command.   25

DOCTOR   You see her eyes are open.

GENTLEWOMAN   Ay, but their sense are shut.

DOCTOR   What is it she does now? Look how she rubs
her hands.

GENTLEWOMAN   It is an accustomed action with her to   30
seem thus washing her hands. I have known her
continue in this a quarter of an hour.

LADY MACBETH   Yet here's a spot.

DOCTOR   Hark, she speaks. I will set down what comes
from her, to satisfy my remembrance the more   35
strongly.

LADY MACBETH   Out, damned spot, out, I say! One. Two.
Why then, 'tis time to do 't. Hell is murky. Fie, my
lord, fie, a soldier and afeard? What need we fear
who knows it, when none can call our power to   40
account? Yet who would have thought the old man
to have had so much blood in him?

DOCTOR   Do you mark that?

LADY MACBETH   The Thane of Fife had a wife. Where is
she now? What, will these hands ne'er be clean? No   45
more o' that, my lord, no more o' that. You mar all
with this starting.

DOCTOR   Go to, go to. You have known what you should
not.

GENTLEWOMAN   She has spoke what she should not,   50
I am sure of that. Heaven knows what she has
known.

LADY MACBETH   Here's the smell of the blood still. All
the perfumes of Arabia will not sweeten this little
hand. O, O, O!   55

DOCTOR   What a sigh is there! The heart is sorely
charged.

GENTLEWOMAN   I would not have such a heart in my
bosom for the dignity of the whole body.

67. **on 's:** of his
78. **divine:** minister or priest
80. **annoyance:** i.e., injuring herself
82. **mated:** stupefied

5.2 A Scottish force, in rebellion against Macbeth, marches toward Birnam Wood to join Malcolm and his English army.

---

0 SD. **Drum and Colors:** i.e., a drummer and men carrying banners

A Scottish castle with moat, drawbridge,
and towers. (5.2.14)
From Raphael Holinshed, *The historie of Scotland* (1577).

DOCTOR Well, well, well. 60
GENTLEWOMAN Pray God it be, sir.
DOCTOR This disease is beyond my practice. Yet I have
known those which have walked in their sleep,
who have died holily in their beds.
LADY MACBETH Wash your hands. Put on your night- 65
gown. Look not so pale. I tell you yet again, Ban-
quo's buried; he cannot come out on 's grave.
DOCTOR Even so?
LADY MACBETH To bed, to bed. There's knocking at the
gate. Come, come, come, come. Give me your 70
hand. What's done cannot be undone. To bed, to
bed, to bed. *Lady ⌜Macbeth⌝ exits.*
DOCTOR Will she go now to bed?
GENTLEWOMAN Directly.
DOCTOR
Foul whisp'rings are abroad. Unnatural deeds 75
Do breed unnatural troubles. Infected minds
To their deaf pillows will discharge their secrets.
More needs she the divine than the physician.
God, God forgive us all. Look after her.
Remove from her the means of all annoyance 80
And still keep eyes upon her. So, good night.
My mind she has mated, and amazed my sight.
I think but dare not speak.
GENTLEWOMAN   Good night, good doctor.
They exit.

Scene 2
*Drum and Colors. Enter Menteith, Caithness, Angus,
Lennox, ⌜and⌝ Soldiers.*

MENTEITH
The English power is near, led on by Malcolm,
His uncle Siward, and the good Macduff.

3. **dear:** deeply felt; also, grievous, dire

4–5. **Would . . . man:** i.e., would quicken dead men to bloody and desperate attack **alarm:** call to fight **Excite:** quicken **mortified:** dead

9. **file:** list

11. **unrough:** unbearded, smooth-faced

12. **Protest:** assert; **their first of manhood:** the beginning of their manhood

17. **distempered:** diseased and swollen

21. **minutely:** i.e., every minute; **upbraid:** condemn; **faith-breach:** breach of his oath (to Duncan— or breach of all oaths and vows)

27. **pestered:** infested; obstructed; overcrowded; **to recoil and start:** to flinch in alarm

32. **weal:** state, commonwealth

33–34. **pour . . . us:** i.e., pour out every drop of our blood in purging (curing) our country

Revenges burn in them, for their dear causes
Would to the bleeding and the grim alarm
Excite the mortified man.   5
ANGUS   Near Birnam Wood
Shall we well meet them. That way are they coming.
CAITHNESS
Who knows if Donalbain be with his brother?
LENNOX
For certain, sir, he is not. I have a file
Of all the gentry. There is Siward's son   10
And many unrough youths that even now
Protest their first of manhood.
MENTEITH   What does the tyrant?
CAITHNESS
Great Dunsinane he strongly fortifies.
Some say he's mad; others that lesser hate him   15
Do call it valiant fury. But for certain
He cannot buckle his distempered cause
Within the belt of rule.
ANGUS   Now does he feel
His secret murders sticking on his hands.   20
Now minutely revolts upbraid his faith-breach.
Those he commands move only in command,
Nothing in love. Now does he feel his title
Hang loose about him, like a giant's robe
Upon a dwarfish thief.   25
MENTEITH   Who, then, shall blame
His pestered senses to recoil and start
When all that is within him does condemn
Itself for being there?
CAITHNESS   Well, march we on   30
To give obedience where 'tis truly owed.
Meet we the med'cine of the sickly weal,
And with him pour we in our country's purge
Each drop of us.
LENNOX   Or so much as it needs   35

5.3 Reports are brought to Macbeth of the Scottish and English forces massed against him. He seeks assurance in the apparitions' promise of safety for himself. But he is anxious about Lady Macbeth's condition and impatient with her doctor's inability to cure her.

———

1. **them:** i.e., the deserting thanes
3. **taint:** become tainted
5. **mortal consequences:** that which happens to humanity
9. **English epicures:** a Scottish taunt at English eating habits **epicures:** gluttons, or those devoted to luxury
10. **sway by:** rule myself by
12. **loon:** fool
18. **lily-livered:** white-livered (because bloodless), cowardly; **patch:** fool
19. **of thy:** on your
20. **Are counselors to fear:** i.e., teach others to be frightened
24. **push:** effort

To dew the sovereign flower and drown the weeds.
Make we our march towards Birnam.

> *They exit marching.*

Scene 3
Enter Macbeth, ⌜the⌝ Doctor, and Attendants.

MACBETH
Bring me no more reports. Let them fly all.
Till Birnam Wood remove to Dunsinane
I cannot taint with fear. What's the boy Malcolm?
Was he not born of woman? The spirits that know
All mortal consequences have pronounced me thus: 5
"Fear not, Macbeth. No man that's born of woman
Shall e'er have power upon thee." Then fly, false
    thanes,
And mingle with the English epicures.
The mind I sway by and the heart I bear   10
Shall never sag with doubt nor shake with fear.

> *Enter Servant.*

The devil damn thee black, thou cream-faced loon!
Where got'st thou that goose-look?
SERVANT   There is ten thousand—
MACBETH   Geese, villain?   15
SERVANT   Soldiers, sir.
MACBETH
Go prick thy face and over-red thy fear,
Thou lily-livered boy. What soldiers, patch?
Death of thy soul! Those linen cheeks of thine
Are counselors to fear. What soldiers, whey-face?   20
SERVANT   The English force, so please you.
MACBETH
Take thy face hence.   ⌜*Servant exits.*⌝
                Seyton!—I am sick at heart
When I behold—Seyton, I say!—This push

25. **disseat:** unseat, dethrone
27. **the sere:** the (condition of being) dry and withered
29. **As:** such as
30. **look:** expect
31. **mouth-honor:** honor from the tongue (rather than the heart)
32. **fain:** gladly
42. **Skirr:** search quickly, scour
52. **Raze out:** erase
53. **oblivious:** i.e., causing oblivion
54. **stuffed:** clogged

Will cheer me ever or ⌜disseat⌝ me now.   25
I have lived long enough. My way of life
Is fall'n into the sere, the yellow leaf,
And that which should accompany old age,
As honor, love, obedience, troops of friends,
I must not look to have, but in their stead   30
Curses, not loud but deep, mouth-honor, breath
Which the poor heart would fain deny and dare
   not.—
Seyton!

Enter Seyton.

SEYTON
What's your gracious pleasure?   35
MACBETH   What news more?
SEYTON
All is confirmed, my lord, which was reported.
MACBETH
I'll fight till from my bones my flesh be hacked.
Give me my armor.
SEYTON   'Tis not needed yet.   40
MACBETH   I'll put it on.
Send out more horses. Skirr the country round.
Hang those that talk of fear. Give me mine
   armor.—
How does your patient, doctor?   45
DOCTOR   Not so sick, my lord,
As she is troubled with thick-coming fancies
That keep her from her rest.
MACBETH   Cure ⌜her⌝ of that.
Canst thou not minister to a mind diseased,   50
Pluck from the memory a rooted sorrow,
Raze out the written troubles of the brain,
And with some sweet oblivious antidote
Cleanse the stuffed bosom of that perilous stuff
Which weighs upon the heart?   55

58. **physic:** medicine

62. **dispatch:** make haste (probably said to one of his attendants who is arming him)

62–63. **cast / The water of my land:** i.e., diagnose the disease from which Scotland is suffering **cast the water:** examine the (patient's) urine to diagnose an illness

69. **them:** i.e., the English

73. **bane:** destruction

5.4 The rebel Scottish forces have joined Malcolm's army at Birnam Wood. Malcolm orders each soldier to cut down and carry a bough from the wood so as to conceal their numbers from Macbeth.

----

1. **Cousins:** kinsmen

2. **chambers:** i.e., such rooms as bedchambers and dining rooms (see 1.7.31)

DOCTOR   Therein the patient
  Must minister to himself.

MACBETH
  Throw physic to the dogs. I'll none of it.—
  Come, put mine armor on. Give me my staff.
              ⌜*Attendants begin to arm him.*⌝
  Seyton, send out.—Doctor, the thanes fly from   60
    me.—
  Come, sir, dispatch.—If thou couldst, doctor, cast
  The water of my land, find her disease,
  And purge it to a sound and pristine health,
  I would applaud thee to the very echo   65
  That should applaud again.—Pull 't off, I say.—
  What rhubarb, senna, or what purgative drug
  Would scour these English hence? Hear'st thou of
    them?

DOCTOR
  Ay, my good lord. Your royal preparation   70
  Makes us hear something.

MACBETH   Bring it after me.—
  I will not be afraid of death and bane
  Till Birnam Forest come to Dunsinane.

DOCTOR, ⌜*aside*⌝
  Were I from Dunsinane away and clear,   75
  Profit again should hardly draw me here.
                       They exit.

Scene 4
Drum and Colors. Enter Malcolm, Siward, Macduff,
Siward's son, Menteith, Caithness, Angus, and Soldiers,
marching.

MALCOLM
  Cousins, I hope the days are near at hand
  That chambers will be safe.

3. **nothing:** not at all

7. **shadow:** conceal

8. **host:** army; **discovery:** i.e., Macbeth's scouts or sentinels

11. **no other but:** nothing else but that

12. **Keeps:** remains

12–13. **endure . . . before 't:** not prevent our laying siege to it

15. **where . . . given:** i.e., wherever opportunity offers itself

16. **more and less:** nobles and commoners

19–20. **Let . . . event:** i.e., let us wait to judge until we see the outcome **censures:** judgments **Attend:** await **true event:** actual outcome

24. **owe:** (actually) own, possess

26. **certain issue strokes must arbitrate:** i.e., the definite outcome must be decided by blows

MENTEITH   We doubt it nothing.
SIWARD
  What wood is this before us?
MENTEITH   The wood of Birnam.   5
MALCOLM
  Let every soldier hew him down a bough
  And bear 't before him. Thereby shall we shadow
  The numbers of our host and make discovery
  Err in report of us.
SOLDIER   It shall be done.   10
SIWARD
  We learn no other but the confident tyrant
  Keeps still in Dunsinane and will endure
  Our setting down before 't.
MALCOLM   'Tis his main hope;
  For, where there is advantage to be given,   15
  Both more and less have given him the revolt,
  And none serve with him but constrainèd things
  Whose hearts are absent too.
MACDUFF   Let our just censures
  Attend the true event, and put we on   20
  Industrious soldiership.
SIWARD   The time approaches
  That will with due decision make us know
  What we shall say we have and what we owe.
  Thoughts speculative their unsure hopes relate,   25
  But certain issue strokes must arbitrate;
  Towards which, advance the war.
                          They exit marching.

5.5   Macbeth is confident that he can withstand any siege from Malcolm's forces. He is then told of Lady Macbeth's death and of the apparent movement of Birnam Wood toward Dunsinane Castle, where he waits. He desperately resolves to abandon the castle and give battle to Malcolm in the field.

————

4. **ague:** pestilence (pronounced *a-gue*)

5. **forced:** reinforced; also, perhaps, stuffed ("farced")

5–6. **those that should be ours:** i.e., deserters from our ranks

7. **met them:** i.e., in the field, in open battle; **dareful:** boldly

12. **my . . . cooled:** I would have been chilled

13. **my fell of hair:** i.e., the hair on my scalp

14. **dismal treatise:** dreadful tale

15. **As:** as if

16. **Direness:** horror

17. **start:** startle

18. **Wherefore:** for what reason, why

20. **She should have died hereafter:** i.e., she would inevitably have died sometime; or, perhaps, she ought to have died later

22–26. **Tomorrow . . . death:** Behind Macbeth's terrible reflections lie the images of "life as a story" and "life as light" as in Matthew 5.16. See also Psalms 22.15, 39.6, 90.9; Job 14.1–2, 18.6.

23. **petty:** slow, insignificant

24. **recorded time:** i.e., recordable time

26. **dusty death:** See Genesis 3.19: "for dust thou art, and unto dust shalt thou return."

Scene 5

Enter Macbeth, Seyton, and Soldiers, with Drum and
Colors.

MACBETH
Hang out our banners on the outward walls.
The cry is still "They come!" Our castle's strength
Will laugh a siege to scorn. Here let them lie
Till famine and the ague eat them up.
Were they not forced with those that should be   5
  ours,
We might have met them dareful, beard to beard,
And beat them backward home.
                              A cry within of women.
                        What is that noise?

SEYTON
It is the cry of women, my good lord.   ⌜*He exits.*⌝   10
MACBETH
I have almost forgot the taste of fears.
The time has been my senses would have cooled
To hear a night-shriek, and my fell of hair
Would at a dismal treatise rouse and stir
As life were in 't. I have supped full with horrors.   15
Direness, familiar to my slaughterous thoughts,
Cannot once start me.

⌜*Enter Seyton.*⌝

                        Wherefore was that cry?
SEYTON   The Queen, my lord, is dead.
MACBETH   She should have died hereafter.   20
There would have been a time for such a word.
Tomorrow and tomorrow and tomorrow
Creeps in this petty pace from day to day
To the last syllable of recorded time,
And all our yesterdays have lighted fools   25
The way to dusty death. Out, out, brief candle!

27. **shadow:** image without substance; also, actor; **player:** actor

38. **anon:** soon

46. **cling:** wither, shrink; **speech be sooth:** story is true

48. **pull in:** i.e., rein in; **resolution:** determination, steadfastness

49. **doubt:** suspect

54. **nor . . . nor:** neither . . . nor

56. **th' estate o' th' world:** perhaps, the settled order of the universe

57. **undone:** destroyed

Life's but a walking shadow, a poor player
That struts and frets his hour upon the stage
And then is heard no more. It is a tale
Told by an idiot, full of sound and fury,   30
Signifying nothing.

Enter a Messenger.

Thou com'st to use thy tongue: thy story quickly.
MESSENGER   Gracious my lord,
  I should report that which I say I saw,
  But know not how to do 't.   35
MACBETH   Well, say, sir.
MESSENGER
  As I did stand my watch upon the hill,
  I looked toward Birnam, and anon methought
  The wood began to move.
MACBETH   Liar and slave!   40
MESSENGER
  Let me endure your wrath, if 't be not so.
  Within this three mile may you see it coming.
  I say, a moving grove.
MACBETH   If thou speak'st false,
  Upon the next tree shall thou hang alive   45
  Till famine cling thee. If thy speech be sooth,
  I care not if thou dost for me as much.—
  I pull in resolution and begin
  To doubt th' equivocation of the fiend,
  That lies like truth. "Fear not till Birnam Wood   50
  Do come to Dunsinane," and now a wood
  Comes toward Dunsinane.—Arm, arm, and out!—
  If this which he avouches does appear,
  There is nor flying hence nor tarrying here.
  I 'gin to be aweary of the sun   55
  And wish th' estate o' th' world were now
    undone.—

58. **alarum bell:** the bell that calls to arms; **wrack:** ruin, destruction
59. **harness:** i.e., armor

5.6 Malcolm arrives with his troops before Dunsinane Castle.

———

2. **uncle:** addressed to Siward
4. **battle:** battalion, main body; **we:** Note that Malcolm here uses the royal "we."
8. **power:** army
11. **harbingers:** announcers, forerunners

5.7 On the battlefield Macbeth kills young Siward, the son of the English commander. After Macbeth exits, Macduff arrives in search of him. Dunsinane Castle has already been surrendered to Malcolm, whose forces have been strengthened by deserters from Macbeth's army.

———

1–2. **They have . . . course:** Macbeth here sees himself as a bear in a bearbaiting, tied to a stake and set upon by dogs. **course:** attack, encounter

Ring the alarum bell!—Blow wind, come wrack,
At least we'll die with harness on our back.

They exit.

Scene 6

*Drum and Colors. Enter Malcolm, Siward, Macduff, and
their army, with boughs.*

MALCOLM
Now near enough. Your leafy screens throw down
And show like those you are.—You, worthy uncle,
Shall with my cousin, your right noble son,
Lead our first battle. Worthy Macduff and we
Shall take upon 's what else remains to do,   5
According to our order.
SIWARD   Fare you well.
Do we but find the tyrant's power tonight,
Let us be beaten if we cannot fight.
MACDUFF
Make all our trumpets speak; give them all breath,   10
Those clamorous harbingers of blood and death.

They exit.
Alarums continued.

Scene 7

Enter Macbeth.

MACBETH
They have tied me to a stake. I cannot fly,
But, bear-like, I must fight the course. What's he
That was not born of woman? Such a one
Am I to fear, or none.

Enter young Siward.

YOUNG SIWARD   What is thy name?   5

10. **title:** name

14. **prove:** challenge, test

21. **still:** always

22. **kerns:** i.e., hired soldiers (more specifically, Irish foot soldiers)

23. **staves:** weapons; **Either thou:** i.e., either I find you

25. **undeeded:** i.e., unused

26–27. **one . . . bruited:** someone of great reputation is proclaimed

29. **gently rendered:** surrendered without a fight

A bear "tied to a stake." (5.7.1)
From Giacomo Franco, *Habiti d'huomeni* . . . (1609?).

MACBETH   Thou'lt be afraid to hear it.
YOUNG SIWARD
  No, though thou call'st thyself a hotter name
  Than any is in hell.
MACBETH   My name's Macbeth.
YOUNG SIWARD
  The devil himself could not pronounce a title   10
  More hateful to mine ear.
MACBETH   No, nor more fearful.
YOUNG SIWARD
  Thou liest, abhorrèd tyrant. With my sword
  I'll prove the lie thou speak'st.
            ⌐They¬ *fight, and young Siward* ⌐is¬ *slain.*
MACBETH   Thou wast born of   15
    woman.
  But swords I smile at, weapons laugh to scorn,
  Brandished by man that's of a woman born.
                                        He exits.

            Alarums. Enter Macduff.

MACDUFF
  That way the noise is. Tyrant, show thy face!
  If thou beest slain, and with no stroke of mine,   20
  My wife and children's ghosts will haunt me still.
  I cannot strike at wretched kerns, whose arms
  Are hired to bear their staves. Either thou, Macbeth,
  Or else my sword with an unbattered edge
  I sheathe again undeeded. There thou shouldst be;   25
  By this great clatter, one of greatest note
  Seems bruited. Let me find him, Fortune,
  And more I beg not.   *He exits. Alarums.*

            Enter Malcolm and Siward.

SIWARD
  This way, my lord. The castle's gently rendered.
  The tyrant's people on both sides do fight,   30

32. **itself professes:** announces itself

35. **strike beside us:** i.e., fight on our side, side by side

5.8 Macduff finds Macbeth, who is reluctant to fight with him because Macbeth has already killed Macduff's whole family and is sure of killing Macduff too if they fight. When Macduff announces that he is not, strictly speaking, a man born of woman, having been ripped prematurely from his mother's womb, then Macbeth is afraid to fight. He fights with Macduff only when Macduff threatens to capture him and display him as a public spectacle. Macduff kills Macbeth, cuts off his head, and brings it to Malcolm. With Macbeth dead, Malcolm is now king and gives new titles to his loyal supporters.

———————

1. **Roman:** associated here with approval of suicide

2. **lives:** i.e., others living

6. **charged:** burdened

10. **Than terms can give thee out:** i.e., than words can describe you

12. **intrenchant:** invulnerable, unable to be cut

13. **impress:** leave a mark on

18. **angel:** i.e., evil spirit; **still:** always

20. **Untimely:** prematurely

The noble thanes do bravely in the war,
The day almost itself professes yours,
And little is to do.
MALCOLM   We have met with foes
That strike beside us.   35
SIWARD   Enter, sir, the castle.
                                   They exit. Alarum.

⌈Scene 8⌉
Enter Macbeth.

MACBETH
Why should I play the Roman fool and die
On mine own sword? Whiles I see lives, the gashes
Do better upon them.

Enter Macduff.

MACDUFF   Turn, hellhound, turn!
MACBETH
Of all men else I have avoided thee.   5
But get thee back. My soul is too much charged
With blood of thine already.
MACDUFF   I have no words;
My voice is in my sword, thou bloodier villain
Than terms can give thee out.   *Fight. Alarum.*   10
MACBETH   Thou losest labor.
As easy mayst thou the intrenchant air
With thy keen sword impress as make me bleed.
Let fall thy blade on vulnerable crests;
I bear a charmèd life, which must not yield   15
To one of woman born.
MACDUFF   Despair thy charm,
And let the angel whom thou still hast served
Tell thee Macduff was from his mother's womb
Untimely ripped.   20

22. **my better part of man:** the better part of my manhood (i.e., perhaps, courage)

23. **juggling:** deceiving

24. **palter . . . sense:** trick us by using words ambiguously

28. **gaze:** that which is gazed at; spectacle

30. **Painted upon a pole:** i.e., his picture painted and displayed on a pole, as for a sideshow; **underwrit:** written underneath

34. **baited:** attacked from all sides (as the bear is in a bearbaiting)

36. **opposed:** i.e., my opponent

39 SD. **They enter fighting, and Macbeth is slain:** This Folio stage direction is omitted by many editors because they feel that it contradicts the stage direction that immediately precedes it in the Folio: *"Exit fighting. Alarums."* Although early printed texts such as the Folio sometimes include duplicatory or contradictory stage directions, it is certainly possible in this case to perform all the directions printed in the Folio and reprinted here.

40. **miss:** lack

41. **go off:** i.e., die; **by these:** to judge by those present

MACBETH
Accursèd be that tongue that tells me so,
For it hath cowed my better part of man!
And be these juggling fiends no more believed
That palter with us in a double sense,
That keep the word of promise to our ear   25
And break it to our hope. I'll not fight with thee.
MACDUFF   Then yield thee, coward,
And live to be the show and gaze o' th' time.
We'll have thee, as our rarer monsters are,
Painted upon a pole, and underwrit   30
"Here may you see the tyrant."
MACBETH   I will not yield
To kiss the ground before young Malcolm's feet
And to be baited with the rabble's curse.
Though Birnam Wood be come to Dunsinane   35
And thou opposed, being of no woman born,
Yet I will try the last. Before my body
I throw my warlike shield. Lay on, Macduff,
And damned be him that first cries "Hold! Enough!"
                              They exit fighting. Alarums.

⌜*They*⌝ *enter fighting, and Macbeth* ⌜*is*⌝ *slain.* ⌜*Macduff
exits carrying off Macbeth's body.*⌝ *Retreat and flourish.
Enter, with Drum and Colors, Malcolm, Siward, Ross,
Thanes, and Soldiers.*

MALCOLM
I would the friends we miss were safe arrived.   40
SIWARD
Some must go off; and yet by these I see
So great a day as this is cheaply bought.
MALCOLM
Macduff is missing, and your noble son.
ROSS
Your son, my lord, has paid a soldier's debt.
He only lived but till he was a man,   45

47. **unshrinking . . . fought:** where he fought steadfastly, refusing to give ground

53. **before:** on the front of his body

67. **compassed . . . pearl:** surrounded by the most choice subjects of your kingdom

73–74. **reckon . . . even with you:** make an accounting of (also, take into account) the love each of you has shown, and discharge my debt to you

The which no sooner had his prowess confirmed
In the unshrinking station where he fought,
But like a man he died.
SIWARD   Then he is dead?
ROSS
　Ay, and brought off the field. Your cause of sorrow   50
　Must not be measured by his worth, for then
　It hath no end.
SIWARD   Had he his hurts before?
ROSS
　Ay, on the front.
SIWARD   Why then, God's soldier be he!   55
　Had I as many sons as I have hairs,
　I would not wish them to a fairer death;
　And so his knell is knolled.
MALCOLM
　He's worth more sorrow, and that I'll spend for
　　him.   60
SIWARD　He's worth no more.
　They say he parted well and paid his score,
　And so, God be with him. Here comes newer
　　comfort.

　　　Enter Macduff with Macbeth's head.

MACDUFF
　Hail, King! for so thou art. Behold where stands   65
　Th' usurper's cursèd head. The time is free.
　I see thee compassed with thy kingdom's pearl,
　That speak my salutation in their minds,
　Whose voices I desire aloud with mine.
　Hail, King of Scotland!   70
ALL　Hail, King of Scotland!   *Flourish.*
MALCOLM
　We shall not spend a large expense of time
　Before we reckon with your several loves
　And make us even with you. My thanes and
　　kinsmen,   75

78. **Which . . . time:** which should be done immediately in this new era

79. **As:** such as

81. **Producing . . . ministers:** bringing forth (to
justice) the agents

83. **self and violent hands:** her own violent hands

Henceforth be earls, the first that ever Scotland
In such an honor named. What's more to do,
Which would be planted newly with the time,
As calling home our exiled friends abroad
That fled the snares of watchful tyranny,   80
Producing forth the cruel ministers
Of this dead butcher and his fiend-like queen
(Who, as 'tis thought, by self and violent hands,
Took off her life)—this, and what needful else
That calls upon us, by the grace of grace,   85
We will perform in measure, time, and place.
So thanks to all at once and to each one,
Whom we invite to see us crowned at Scone.

Flourish. All exit.

Textual Notes

The reading of the present text appears to the left of the square bracket. The earliest sources of readings not in **F**, the First Folio text (upon which this edition is based), are indicated as follows: **F2** is the Second Folio of 1632; **F3** is the Third Folio of 1663-64; **F4** is the Fourth Folio of 1685; **Ed.** is an earlier editor of Shakespeare, beginning with Rowe in 1709. No sources are given for emendations of punctuation or for corrections of obvious typographical errors, like turned letters that produce no known word. **SD** means stage direction; **SP** means speech prefix; **uncorr.** means the first or uncorrected state of the First Folio; **corr.** means the second or corrected state of the First Folio; ~ stands in place of a word already quoted before the square bracket; ˄ indicates the omission of a punctuation mark.

1.1   10–11. SP SECOND WITCH . . . THIRD WITCH] Ed.;
            All F
        10. calls.] ~ ˄ F
1.2   0. SD *King Duncan, Malcolm*] Ed.; *King
            Malcolme* F
         1 *and throughout play* SP DUNCAN] Ed.;
            King. F
        15. gallowglasses] F2; Gallowgrosses F
        16. quarrel] Ed.; Quarry F
        28. break] Ed.; *omit* F
1.3   40. Forres] Ed.; Soris F
        100. make,] ~ ˄ F
        102. Came] Ed.; Can F
1.4   1. Are] F2; Or F
1.5   1 *and throughout play* SP LADY MACBETH]
            Ed.; Lady. F
        37–38. him, . . . preparation?] ~? . . . ~. F

74. matters. To . . . time,] ~, ~ . . . ~. F

1.6   5. martlet] Ed.; Barlet F

6. mansionry] Ed.; Mansonry F

7. jutty,] ~ ˄ F

10. most] Ed.; must F

37. host.] ~ ˄ F

1.7   5. end-all ˄] ~ ˄ ~. F

6. shoal] Ed.; Schoole F

47–49. esteem, . . . adage?] ~? . . . ~. F

52. do] Ed.; no F

81–82. officers, . . . quell?] ~? . . . ~. F

2.1   67. strides] Ed.; sides F

69. sure] Ed.; sowre F

70. way they] Ed.; they may F

2.2   17. SD *after line 11 in* F

93. SD *after "deed" in* F

2.3   0. SD *Knocking within. Enter a Porter.*] Ed.;
            Enter a Porter. Knocking within. F

20. SD *The . . . Lennox.*] this ed.; *Enter Mac-
            duffe and Lenox.* F *1 line later*

44. SD *1 line earlier in* F

84. SD *1 line later in* F

159. SD *All . . . exit.*] Ed.; *Exeunt.* F

2.4   52. Well,] ~ ˄ F

3.1   10. SD *Lady Macbeth, Lennox*] Ed.; *Lady
            Lenox* F

45–46. night. . . . welcome,] ~, . . . ~: F

81, 131, 159. SP MURDERERS] Ed.; *Murth.* F

118. heart ˄] ~; F

162. SD *He exits.*] Ed.; *Exeunt.* F

3.3   9. and] F2; end F

3.4   10. thanks.] ~ ˄ F

94. time] Ed.; times F

144. worse.] ~ ˄ F

167. worst.] ~, F

176. in deed] F (indeed)

3.6	28. son] Ed.; Sonnes F
	42. the] Ed.; their F
	50. t' hold] F2; t hold F
4.1	5. throw.] ~ ˄ F
	38. SD *to*] Ed.; *and* F
	62. germens . . . all together] Ed.; Germaine . . . altogether F
	83. thanks.] ~ ˄ F
	94. assurance ˄] ~: F
	107. SD *He descends.*] Ed.; *Descend.* F
	120. SD *1 line later in* F
	126. SD *A . . . last.*] this ed.; *A shew of eight Kings, and Banquo last, with a glasse in his hand.* F
	134. eighth] F (eight)
4.2	1 *and throughout scene* SP LADY MACDUFF] Ed.; *Wife* F
	75. ones!] ~ ˄ F
	76. thus ˄] ~. F
	87. SD *1 line later in* F
	89 *and throughout scene* SP MURDERER] Ed.; *Mur.* F
	98. SD *Lady . . . body.*] Ed.; *Exit crying Murther.* F
4.3	5. downfall'n] Ed.; downfall F
	18. deserve] Ed.; discerne F
33–35.	child, . . . leave-taking?] ~? . . . ~-~. F
	43. affeered] F (affear'd)
	125. accursed] F2; accust F
	142. detraction,] ~. F
	146. own,] ~. F
	152. thy] F2; they F
	152. here-approach] Ed.; ~ ˄ ~ F
	166. SD *1 line earlier in* F
	176. on with] F *corr.;* on my with F *uncorr.*
	183. not] F2; nor F

199. relation⌃]~; F
251. SP ROSS] F *corr.; Roffe.* F *uncorr.*
273. myself.] ~ ⌃ F
276. tune] Ed.; time F
5.3   25. disseat] Ed.; dis-eate F
49. her] F2; *omit* F
64. pristine] F2; pristiue F
5.4   10. SP SOLDIER] Ed.; *Sold.* F
5.5   8. SD *1 line later in* F
44. false] F2; fhlse F

Macbeth:
A Modern Perspective
Susan Snyder

Coleridge pronounced *Macbeth* to be "wholly tragic." Rejecting the drunken Porter of Act 2, scene 3 as "an interpolation of the actors," and perceiving no wordplay in the rest of the text (he was wrong on both counts), he declared that the play had no comic admixture at all. More acutely, though still in support of this sense of the play as unadulterated tragedy, he noted the absence in *Macbeth* of a process characteristic of other Shakespearean tragedies, the "reasonings of equivocal morality."[1]

Indeed, as Macbeth ponders his decisive tragic act of killing the king, he is not deceived about its moral nature. To kill anyone to whom he is tied by obligations of social and political loyalty as well as kinship is, he knows, deeply wrong:

> He's here in double trust:
> First, as I am his kinsman and his subject,
> Strong both against the deed; then, as his host,
> Who should against his murderer shut the door,
> Not bear the knife myself.   (1.7.12–16)

And to kill Duncan, who has been "so clear in his great office" (that is, so free from corruption as a ruler), is to compound the iniquity. In adapting the story of Macbeth from Holinshed's *Chronicles of Scotland*, Shakespeare created a stark black-white moral opposition by omitting from his story Duncan's weakness as a monarch while retaining his gentle, virtuous nature. Unlike his prototype in Holinshed's history, Macbeth kills not an ineffective leader but a saint whose benevolent presence blesses Scotland. In the same vein of polarized morality, Shakespeare departs from the Holinshed account in which Macbeth is joined in regicide by Banquo and others; instead, he has Macbeth act alone against Duncan. While it might be good politics to distance Banquo from guilt (he was an ancestor of James I, the current king of England and patron of Shakespeare's acting company), excluding the other thanes as well suggests that the playwright had decided to focus on private, purely moral issues uncomplicated by the gray shades of political expediency.

Duncan has done nothing, then, to deserve violent death. Unlike such tragic heroes as Brutus and Othello who are enmeshed in "equivocal morality," Macbeth cannot justify his actions by the perceived misdeeds of his victim. "I have no spur," he admits, "To prick the sides of my intent, but only / Vaulting ambition" (1.7.25–27). This ambition is portrayed indirectly rather than directly. But it is surely no accident that the Weïrd Sisters accost him and crystallize his secret thoughts of the crown into objective possibility just when he has hit new heights of success captaining Duncan's armies and defeating Duncan's enemies. The element of displacement and substitution here—Macbeth leading the fight for Scotland while the titular leader waits behind the lines for the outcome—reinforces our sense that, whatever mysterious timetable the Sisters work by, this is the psychologically right moment to confront Macbeth with their predictions of greatness. Hailed as thane of Glamis, thane of Cawdor, and king, he is initially curious and disbelieving. Though his first fearful reaction (1.3.54) is left unexplained, for us to fill in as we will, surely one way to read his fear is that the word "king" touches a buried nerve of desire. When Ross and Angus immediately arrive to announce that Macbeth is now Cawdor as well as Glamis, the balance of skepticism tilts precipitously toward belief. The nerve vibrates intensely. Two-thirds of the prophecy is already accomplished. The remaining prediction, "king hereafter," is suddenly isolated and highlighted; and because of the Sisters' now proven powers of foreknowledge, it seems to call out for its parallel, inevitable fulfillment.

The Weïrd Sisters present nouns rather than verbs. They put titles on Macbeth without telling what actions he must carry out to attain those titles. It is Lady Macbeth who supplies the verbs. Understanding that her husband is torn between the now-articulated object of desire and the fearful deed that must achieve it ("wouldst not play false / And yet wouldst wrongly win," 1.5.22–23), she persuades him by harping relentlessly on manly *action*. That very gap between noun and verb, the desired prize and the doing necessary to win it, becomes a way of taunting him as a coward: "Art thou afeard / To be the same in thine own act and valor / As thou art in desire?" (1.7.43–45). A man is one who closes this gap by strong action, by taking what he wants; whatever inhibits that action is unmanly fear. And a man is one who does what he has sworn to do, no matter what. We never see Macbeth vow to kill Duncan, but in Lady Macbeth's mind just his broaching the subject has become a commitment. With graphic horror she fantasizes how she would tear her nursing baby from her breast and dash its brains out if she had sworn as she says her husband did. She would, that is, violate her deepest nature as a woman, and sever violently the closest tie of kinship and dependence. Till now, Macbeth has resisted such violation, clinging to a more humane definition of "man" that accepts fidelity and obligation as necessary limits on his prowess. Now, in danger of being bested by his wife in this contest of fierce determinations, he accepts her simpler, more primitive equation of manhood with killing: he commits himself to destroying Duncan. It is significant for the lack of "equivocal morality" that even Lady Macbeth in this crucial scene of persuasion doesn't try to manipulate or blur the polarized moral scheme. Adopting instead a warrior ethic apart from social morality, she presents the murder not as good but as heroic.

Moral clarity informs not only the decisions and actions of *Macbeth* but the stage of nature on which they are played out. The natural universe revealed in the play is essentially attuned to the good, so that it reacts to the unambiguously evil act of killing Duncan with disruptions that are equally easy to read. There are wild winds, an earthquake, "strange screams of death" (2.3.61–69). And beyond such general upheaval there is a series of unnatural acts that distortedly mirror Macbeth's. Duncan's horses overthrow natural order and devour each other, like Macbeth turning on his king and cousin. "A falcon, tow'ring in her pride of place"—the monarch of birds at its highest pitch—is killed by a mousing owl, a lesser bird who ordinarily preys on insignificant creatures (2.4.15–16). Most ominous of all, on the morning following the king's death, is the absence of the sun: like the falcon a symbol of monarchy, but expanding that to suggest the source of all life. In a general sense, the sunless day shows the heavens "troubled with man's act" (2.4.7), but the following grim metaphor points to a closer and more sinister connection: "dark night strangles the traveling lamp" (2.4.9). The daylight has been murdered like Duncan. Scotland's moral darkness lasts till the end of Macbeth's reign. The major scenes take place at night or in the atmosphere of the "black, and midnight hags" (4.1.48), and there is no mention of light or sunshine except in England (4.3.1).

Later in the play, nature finds equally fitting forms for its revenge against Macbeth. Despite his violations of the

natural order, he nevertheless expects the laws of nature
to work for him in the usual way. But the next victim,
Banquo, though his murderer has left him "safe in a
ditch" (3.4.28), refuses to stay safely still and out of
sight. In Macbeth's horrified response to this restless
corpse, we may hear not only panic but outrage at the
breakdown of the laws of motion:

> The time has been
> That, when the brains were out, the man would die,
> And there an end. But now they rise again
> With twenty mortal murders on their crowns
> And push us from our stools. This is more strange
> Than such a murder is.   (3.4.94–99)

His word choice is odd: "*they* rise," a plural where we
would expect "he rises," and the loaded word "crowns"
for heads. Macbeth seems to be haunted by his last
victim, King Duncan, as well as the present one. And by
his outraged comparison at the end—the violent death
and the ghostly appearance compete in strangeness—
Macbeth suggests, without consciously intending to,
that Banquo's walking in death answers to, or even is
caused by, the murder that cut him off so prematurely.
The unnatural murder generates unnatural movement
in the dead. Lady Macbeth, too, walks when she should
be immobile in sleep, "a great perturbation in nature"
(5.1.10).

It is through this same ironic trust in natural law that
Macbeth draws strength from the Sisters' later prophecy: if he is safe until Birnam Wood come to Dunsinane,
he must be safe forever.

> Who can impress the forest, bid the tree
> Unfix his earthbound root? Sweet bodements, good!
> Rebellious dead, rise never till the wood
> Of Birnam rise . . .   (4.1.109–12)

His security is ironic because for Macbeth, of all people, there can be no dependence on predictable natural processes. The "rebellious dead" have already unnaturally risen once; fixed trees can move against him as well. And so, in time, they do. Outraged nature keeps matching the Macbeths' transgressions, undoing and expelling their perversities with its own.

In tragedies where right and wrong are rendered problematic, the dramatic focus is likely to be on the complications of choice. *Macbeth,* on the contrary, is preoccupied less with the protagonist's initial choice of a relatively unambiguous wrong action than with the moral decline that follows. H. B. Charlton noted that one could see in *Richard III* as well as *Macbeth* the biblical axiom that "the wages of sin is death"; but where the history play *assumes* the principle, *Macbeth* demonstrates why it has to be that way.[2] The necessity is not so much theological as psychological: we watch in Macbeth the hardening and distortion that follows on self-violation. The need to suppress part of himself in order to kill Duncan becomes a refusal to acknowledge his deed ("I am afraid to think what I have done. / Look on 't again I dare not": 2.2.66–67). His later murders are all done by proxy, in an attempt to create still more distance between the destruction he wills and full psychic awareness of his responsibility. At the same time, murder becomes a necessary activity, the verb now a compulsion almost without regard to the object: plotted after he has seen the Weïrd Sisters' apparitions, Macbeth's attack on Macduff's "line" (4.1.174) is an insane double displacement, of fear of Macduff himself and fury at the vision of the line of kings fathered by Banquo.

Yet the moral universe of *Macbeth* is not as uncomplicated as some critics have imagined. To see in the play's human and physical nature only a straightforward pattern of sin and punishment is to gloss over the questions it raises obliquely, the moral complexities and mysteries it opens up. The Weïrd Sisters, for example, remain undefined. Where do they come from? Where do they go when they disappear from the action in Act 4? What is their place in a moral universe that ostensibly recoils against sin and punishes it? Are they human witches or supernatural beings? Labeling them "evil" seems not so much incorrect as inadequate. Do they cause men to commit crimes or do they only present the possibility to them? Macbeth responds to his prophecy by killing his king, but Banquo after hearing the one directed at him is not impelled to act at all. Do we take this difference as demonstrating that the Sisters have in themselves no power beyond suggestion? Or should we rather find it somewhat sinister later on when Banquo, ancestor of James I or not, sees reason in Macbeth's success to look forward to his own—yet feels it necessary to conceal his hopes (3.1.1–10)?

Even what we most take for granted becomes problematic when scrutinized. Does Macbeth really desire to be king? Lady Macbeth says he does, but what comes through in 1.5 and 1.7 is more her desire than his. Apart from one brief reference to ambition when he is ruling out other motives to kill Duncan, Macbeth himself is strangely silent about any longing for royal power and position. Instead of an obsession that fills his personal horizon, we find in Macbeth something of a motivational void. Why does he feel obligated, or compelled, to bring about an advance in station that the prophecy seems to render inevitable anyway? A. C. Bradley put his finger on this absence of positive desire when he observed that Macbeth commits his crime as if it were "an appalling duty."[3]

Recent lines of critical inquiry also call old certainties into question. Duncan's saintly status would seem as-

sured, yet sociological critics are disquieted by the way
we are introduced to him, as he receives news of the
battle in 1.2. On the one hand we hear reports of
horrifying savagery in the fighting, savagery in which the
loyal thanes participate as much as the rebels and
invaders—more so, in fact, when Macbeth and Banquo
are likened to the crucifiers of Christ ("or memorize
another Golgotha," 1.2.44). In response we see Duncan
exulting not only in the victory but in the bloodshed,
equating honor with wounds. It is not that he bears any
particular guilt. Yet the mild paternal king is nevertheless implicated here in his society's violent warrior
ethic, its predicating of manly worth on prowess in
killing.[4] But isn't this just what we condemn in Lady
Macbeth? Cultural analysis tends to blur the sharp
demarcations, even between two such figures apparently totally opposed, and to draw them together as partici-
pants in and products of the same constellation of social
values.

Lady Macbeth and Duncan meet in a more particular
way, positioned as they are on the same side of Scotland's basic division between warriors and those protected by warriors. The king is too old and fragile to
fight; the lady is neither, but she is barred from battle by
traditional gender conventions that assign her instead
the functions of following her husband's commands and
nurturing her young. In fact, of course, Lady Macbeth's
actions and outlook thoroughly subvert this ideology, as
she forcefully takes the lead in planning the murder and
shames her husband into joining in by her willingness to
slaughter her own nurseling. It is easy to call Lady
Macbeth "evil," but the label tends to close down
analysis exactly where we ought to probe more deeply.
Macbeth's wife is restless in a social role that in spite of
her formidable courage and energy offers no chance of
independent action and heroic achievement. It is almost

inevitable that she turn to achievement at second hand, through and for her husband. Standing perforce on the sidelines, like Duncan once again, she promotes and cheers the killing.

Other situations, too, may be more complex than at first they seem. Lady Macduff, unlike Lady Macbeth, accepts her womanly function of caring for her children and her nonwarrior status of being protected. But she is not protected. The ideology of gender seems just as destructive from the submissive side as from the rebellious, when Macduff deserts her in order to pursue his political cause against Macbeth in England and there is no husband to stand in the way of the murderers sent by Macbeth. The obedient wife dies, with her cherished son, just as the rebellious, murderous lady will die who consigned her own nursing baby to death. The moral universe of *Macbeth* has room for massive injustice. Traditional critics find Lady Macbeth "unnatural," and even those who do not accept the equation of gender ideology with nature can agree with the condemnation in view of her determined suppression of all bonds of human sympathy. Clear enough. But we get more blurring and crossovers when Macduff's wife calls *him* unnatural. In leaving his family defenseless in Macbeth's dangerous Scotland, he too seems to discount human bonds. His own wife complains bitterly that "he wants the natural touch"; where even the tiny wren will fight for her young against the owl, his flight seems to signify fear rather than natural love (4.2.8–16). Ross's reply, "cruel are the times," while it doesn't console Lady Macduff and certainly doesn't save her, strives to relocate the moral ambiguity of Macduff's conduct in the situation created by Macbeth's tyrannical rule. The very political crisis that pulls Macduff away from his family on public business puts his private life in jeopardy through the same act of desertion. But while acknowledging the peculiar tensions raised by a tyrant-king, we may also see in the Macduff family's disaster a tragic version of a more familiar conflict: the contest between public and private commitments that can rack conventional marriages, with the wife confined to a private role while the husband is supposed to balance obligations in both spheres.

Malcolm is allied with Duncan by lineage and with Macduff by their shared role of redemptive champion in the final movement of the play. He, too, is not allowed to travel through the action unsullied. After a long absence from the scene following the murder of Duncan, he reappears in England to be sought by Macduff in the crusade against Macbeth. Malcolm is cautious and reserved, and when he does start speaking more freely, what we hear is an astonishing catalogue of self-accusations. He calls himself lustful, avaricious, guilty of every crime and totally lacking in kingly virtues:

> Nay, had I power, I should
> Pour the sweet milk of concord into hell,
> Uproar the universal peace, confound
> All unity on earth.   (4.3.113–16)

Before people became so familiar with Shakespeare's play, I suspect many audiences believed what Malcolm says of himself. Students on first reading still do. Why shouldn't they? He has been absent from the stage for some time, and his only significant action in the early part of the play was to run away after his father's murder. When this essentially unknown prince lists his vices in lengthy speeches of self-loathing, there is no indication—except an exaggeration easily ascribable to his youth—that he is not sincere. And if we do believe, we cannot help joining in Macduff's distress. Malcolm, the last hope for redeeming Scotland from the tyrant, has let us down. Duncan's son is more corrupt than Macbeth. He even sounds like Macbeth, whose own milk of human kindness (1.5.17) was curdled by his wife; who threatened to destroy the whole natural order, "though the treasure / Of nature's germens tumble all together / Even till destruction sicken" (4.1.60–63). In due course, Malcolm takes it all back; but his words once spoken cannot simply be canceled, erased as if they were on paper. We have already, on hearing them, mentally and emotionally processed the false "facts," absorbed them experientially. Perhaps they continue to color indirectly our sense of the next king of Scotland.

Viewed through various lenses, then, the black and white of *Macbeth* may fade toward shades of gray. The play is an open system, offering some fixed markers with which to take one's basic bearings but also, in closer scrutiny, offering provocative questions and moral ambiguities.

----

1. "Notes for a Lecture on *Macbeth*" [c. 1813], in *Coleridge's Writings on Shakespeare*, ed. Terence Hawkes (New York: Capricorn, 1959), p. 188.

2. H. B. Charlton, *Shakespearian Tragedy* (Cambridge: Cambridge University Press, 1948), p. 141.

3. A. C. Bradley, *Shakespearean Tragedy* (London: Macmillan, 1904), p. 358.

4. James L. Calderwood, *If It Were Done: "Macbeth" and Tragic Action* (Amherst: University of Massachusetts Press, 1986), pp. 77–89.

Further Reading

Macbeth

Adelman, Janet. " 'Born of Woman': Fantasies of Maternal Power in *Macbeth.*" In *Cannibals, Witches, and Divorce: Estranging the Renaissance,* edited by Marjorie Garber, pp. 90–121. Baltimore: John Hopkins University Press, 1987.

Focusing on Macbeth's repeated question, "What's he / That was not born of woman?" Adelman argues that *Macbeth* simultaneously represents the fantasy of absolute, destructive maternal power and the male fantasy of absolute escape from this power. Only through the ruthless elimination of all female presence are the primitive fears of male identity ultimately assuaged and contained.

Bradley, A. C. *Shakespearean Tragedy: Lectures on Hamlet, Othello, King Lear, Macbeth* [1904]. London: St. Martin's Press, 1985.

Bradley finds *Macbeth* simpler than Shakespeare's other tragedies, "broader and more massive in effect." He focuses on the psychological makeup of Macbeth and Lady Macbeth, finding that Duncan's murder is a moment of radical change in the protagonists' characters. At that moment, Lady Macbeth loses initiative— "the stem of her being seems to be cut through"—while the opposite occurs with her husband, who "comes into the foreground."

Calderwood, James L. *If It Were Done: "Macbeth" and Tragic Action.* Amherst: University of Massachusetts Press, 1986.

Calderwood addresses *Macbeth* from three different —but not unrelated—perspectives. First, he argues for the play's indebtedness to *Hamlet*, not because of similarities but because the two tragedies are almost systematically opposed. Second, he discusses the play as a tragedy "about the nature of tragedy," finding *Macbeth* to deviate relentlessly from Aristotelian principles of "wholeness, completeness, and limited magnitude." Third, he attempts to show how Shakespeare's play extends into areas of political and social order, reading *Macbeth*'s violence as an eraser of the conventional borders between order and disorder in Scottish society.

Charlton, H. B. *Shakespearian Tragedy*. Cambridge: Cambridge University Press, 1948.

For Charlton, *Macbeth*'s imaginative world is brutal, dominated by night, and pre-Christian, a physical climate in which the characters live according to "a simple, rude and primitive moral code." Charlton examines the tensions existing between Macbeth's "primitive" behavior and his increasing awareness of the nature of evil: "Macbeth appears to stand as a symbol of . . . the moment at which mankind discovered itself to be possessed of capacities for . . . spiritual progress."

Coleridge, S. T. "Notes for a Lecture on *Macbeth*." In *Coleridge's Writings on Shakespeare*, edited by Terence Hawkes, pp. 188–99. New York: Capricorn, 1959.

Coleridge argues that the first appearance of the Weïrd Sisters establishes the "keynote of the character of the whole play." He sets the powerful invocation of the imagination in this scene in contrast to the comparatively mundane opening of *Hamlet*. Coleridge goes on to contrast the openness with which Banquo responds to the Weïrd Sisters with Macbeth's brooding melancholy, concluding that Macbeth has already been tempted by ambitious thoughts.

Garber, Marjorie. *Shakespeare's Ghost Writers: Literature as Uncanny Causality.* London: Methuen, 1987.

Garber explores the ways in which Shakespeare "has come to haunt our culture," whether in literature, history, psychoanalysis, philosophy, or politics. Her chapter on *Macbeth* focuses on the play's self-conception, stage history, and the doubleness of its final tableau. The play's continual disruption of boundaries— "sleepers and forests walk, the dead and the deeds return"—renders *Macbeth* a tragedy that refuses to remain "within the safe boundaries of fiction."

Hawkins, Michael. "History, Politics, and *Macbeth.*" In *Focus on Macbeth,* edited by John Russell Brown, pp. 155–88. London: Routledge & Kegan Paul, 1982.

Examining political questions that concerned Shakespeare's contemporaries, Hawkins discusses how these debates are dealt with in *Macbeth.* He finds *Macbeth* treating four issues in particular: (1) decisive action, commended as likely to bring success in the midst of political uncertainty; (2) Macbeth as a "free agent," that is, the witches notwithstanding, Macbeth is not a pawn of fate; (3) Macbeth as having the political advantage over his opponents in that he knows the future; and (4) Macbeth as successful when following the prophecies, "unsuccessful when he tries to thwart them."

Norbrook, David. "Macbeth and the Politics of Historiography." In *Politics of Discourse: The Literature and History of Seventeenth-Century England,* edited by Kevin Sharpe and Steven Zwicker, pp. 78–116. Berkeley: University of California Press, 1987.

Assuming that Shakespeare was aware of the political

controversies informing the writing of Scottish history, Norbrook sets out the views of major Scottish historians and then demonstrates the ways in which *Macbeth* revises that material. He concludes that the play presents an ambivalent view of Macbeth, for while Macbeth outrages the play's "moral order," some vestiges remain of a worldview in which regicide could be a "noble rather than an evil act."

Sinfield, Alan. "*Macbeth:* History, Ideology and Intellectuals." *Critical Quarterly* 28 (1986): 63–77.

Sinfield points out that the traditional reading of *Macbeth* endorses the use of violence by the absolutist state in order to keep the prevailing political structure in place. For Sinfield, however, *Macbeth* demonstrates that "violence is fundamental in the development of the modern State," concluding that citizens learn to regard state violence as "qualitatively different from other violence and perhaps they don't think of State violence as violence at all."

Stallybrass, Peter. "*Macbeth* and Witchcraft." In *Focus on Macbeth,* edited by John Russell Brown, pp. 189–209. London: Routledge & Kegan Paul, 1982.

Viewing witchcraft in *Macbeth* as an expression of a dominantly patriarchal society, Stallybrass describes both the actual Renaissance beliefs about witches and "the *function* of such beliefs." He concludes that witchcraft as it operates in *Macbeth* serves to confirm the prevailing ideology by moving the debate from the political realm to "the undisputed ground of 'Nature'."

Wheeler, Richard. " 'Since first we were disevered': Trust and Autonomy in Shakespearean Tragedy and Romance." In *Representing Shakespeare: New Psychoanalytic Essays,* edited by Murray M. Schwartz and

Coppélia Kahn, pp. 170–87. Baltimore: Johns Hopkins University Press, 1980.

Wheeler considers Shakespeare's tragedies dramatizations of incompatible modes of self-experience. At one extreme, efforts to establish power are subordinated to a stronger need for a "lost . . . relation of mutuality." At the other extreme, where Wheeler places *Macbeth*, relations that seem to promise fulfillment actually subvert the protagonist's attempt to establish autonomy. Therefore, it is Macbeth's desperate reliance on his powerful wife that ultimately proves to be his undoing.

Shakespeare's Language

Abbott, E. A. *A Shakespearian Grammar*. New York: Haskell House, 1972.

This compact reference book, first published in 1870, helps with many difficulties in Shakespeare's language. It systematically accounts for a host of differences between Shakespeare's usage and sentence structure and our own.

Blake, Norman. *Shakespeare's Language: An Introduction*. New York: St. Martin's Press, 1983.

This general introduction to Elizabethan English discusses various aspects of the language of Shakespeare and his contemporaries, offering possible meanings for hundreds of ambiguous constructions.

Dobson, E. J. *English Pronunciation, 1500–1700*. 2 vols. Oxford: Clarendon Press, 1968.

This long and technical work includes chapters on spelling (and its reformation), phonetics, stressed vowels, and consonants in early modern English.

Houston, John. *Shakespearean Sentences: A Study in Style and Syntax*. Baton Rouge: Louisiana State University Press, 1988.

Houston studies Shakespeare's stylistic choices, considering matters such as sentence length and the relative positions of subject, verb, and direct object. Examining plays throughout the canon in a roughly chronological, developmental order, he analyzes how sentence structure is used in setting tone, in characterization, and for other dramatic purposes.

Onions, C. T. *A Shakespeare Glossary*. Oxford: Clarendon Press, 1986.

This revised edition updates Onions's 1911 standard, selective glossary of words and phrases in Shakespeare's plays that are now obsolete, archaic, or obscure.

Partridge, Eric. *Shakespeare's Bawdy*. London: Routledge & Kegan Paul, 1955.

After an introductory essay, "The Sexual, the Homosexual, and Non-Sexual Bawdy in Shakespeare," Partridge provides a comprehensive glossary of "bawdy" phrases and words from the plays.

Robinson, Randal. *Unlocking Shakespeare's Language: Help for the Teacher and Student*. Urbana, Ill.: National Council of Teachers of English and the ERIC Clearinghouse on Reading and Communication Skills, 1989.

Specifically designed for the high-school and undergraduate college teacher and student, Robinson's book addresses the problems that most often hinder present-day readers of Shakespeare. Through work with his own students, Robinson found that many readers today are particularly puzzled by such stylistic characteristics as subject-verb inversion, interrupted structures, and compression. He shows how our own colloquial language contains comparable structures, and thus helps students recognize such structures when they find them in Shakespeare's plays. This book supplies worksheets—with examples from major plays—to illuminate and remedy such problems as unusual sequences of words and the separation of related parts of sentences.

Shakespeare's Life

Baldwin, T. W. *William Shakspere's Petty School.* Urbana: University of Illinois Press, 1943.

Baldwin here investigates the theory and practice of the petty school, the first level of education in Elizabethan England. He focuses on that educational system primarily as it is reflected in Shakespeare's art.

Baldwin, T. W. *William Shakspere's Small Latine and Lesse Greeke.* 2 vols. Urbana: University of Illinois Press, 1944.

Baldwin attacks the view that Shakespeare was an uneducated genius—a view that had been dominant among Shakespeareans since the eighteenth century. Instead, Baldwin shows, the educational system of Shakespeare's time would have given the playwright a strong background in the classics, and there is much in the plays that shows how Shakespeare benefited from such an education.

Beier, A. L., and Roger Finlay, eds. *London 1500–1700: The Making of the Metropolis.* New York: Longman, 1986.

Focusing on the economic and social history of early modern London, these collected essays probe aspects of metropolitan life, including "Population and Disease,"

"Commerce and Manufacture," and "Society and Change."

Bentley, G. E. *Shakespeare's Life: A Biographical Handbook.* New Haven: Yale University Press, 1961.
This "just-the-facts" account presents the surviving documents of Shakespeare's life against an Elizabethan background.

Chambers, E. K. *William Shakespeare: A Study of Facts and Problems.* 2 vols. Oxford: Clarendon Press, 1930.
Analyzing in great detail the scant historical data, Chambers's complex, scholarly study considers the nature of the texts in which Shakespeare's work is preserved.

Cressy, David. *Education in Tudor and Stuart England.* London: Edward Arnold, 1975.
This volume collects sixteenth-, seventeenth-, and early eighteenth-century documents detailing aspects of formal education in England, such as the curriculum, the control and organization of education, and the education of women.

Dutton, Richard. *William Shakespeare: A Literary Life.* New York: St. Martin's Press, 1989.
Not a biography in the traditional sense, Dutton's very readable work nevertheless "follows the contours of Shakespeare's life" as he examines Shakespeare's career as playwright and poet, with consideration of his patrons, theatrical associations, and audience.

Fraser, Russell. *Young Shakespeare.* New York: Columbia University Press, 1988.

Fraser focuses on Shakespeare's first thirty years, paying attention simultaneously to his life and art.

De Grazia, Margreta. *Shakespeare Verbatim: The Reproduction of Authenticity and the Apparatus of 1790.* Oxford: Clarendon Press, 1991.

De Grazia traces and discusses the development of such editorial criteria as authenticity, historical periodization, factual biography, chronological developments, and close reading, locating as the point of origin Edmond Malone's 1790 edition of Shakespeare's works. There are interesting chapters on the First Folio and on the "legendary" versus the "documented" Shakespeare.

Schoenbaum, S. *William Shakespeare: A Compact Documentary Life.* New York: Oxford University Press, 1977.

This standard biography economically presents the essential documents from Shakespeare's time in an accessible narrative account of the playwright's life.

Shakespeare's Theater

Bentley, G. E. *The Profession of Player in Shakespeare's Time, 1590–1642.* Princeton: Princeton University Press, 1984.

Bentley readably sets forth a wealth of evidence about performance in Shakespeare's time, with special attention to the relations between player and company, and the business of casting, managing, and touring.

Berry, Herbert. *Shakespeare's Playhouses.* New York: AMS Press, 1987.

Berry's six essays collected here discuss (with illustrations) varying aspects of the four playhouses in which

Shakespeare had a financial stake: the Theatre in Shoreditch, the Blackfriars, and the first and second Globe.

Cook, Ann Jennalie. *The Privileged Playgoers of Shakespeare's London*. Princeton: Princeton University Press, 1981.

Cook's work argues, on the basis of sociological, economic, and documentary evidence, that Shakespeare's audience—and the audience for English Renaissance drama generally—consisted mainly of the "privileged."

Greg, W. W. *Dramatic Documents from the Elizabethan Playhouses*. 2 vols. Oxford: Clarendon Press, 1931.

Greg itemizes and briefly describes almost all the play manuscripts that survive from the period 1590 to around 1660, including, among other things, players' parts. His second volume offers facsimiles of selected manuscripts.

Gurr, Andrew. *Playgoing in Shakespeare's London*. Cambridge: Cambridge University Press, 1987.

Gurr charts how the theatrical enterprise developed from its modest beginnings in the 1560s to become a thriving institution in the 1600s. He argues that there were important changes over the period 1567–1644 in the playhouses, the audience, and the plays.

Harbage, Alfred. *Shakespeare's Audience*. New York: Columbia University Press, 1941.

Harbage investigates the fragmentary surviving evidence to interpret the size, composition, and behavior of Shakespeare's audience.

Hattaway, Michael. *Elizabethan Popular Theatre: Plays in Performance*. London: Routledge & Kegan Paul, 1982.

Beginning with a study of the popular drama of the late Elizabethan age—a description of the stages, performance conditions, and acting of the period—this volume concludes with an analysis of five well-known plays of the 1590s, one of them (*Titus Andronicus*) by Shakespeare.

Shapiro, Michael. *Children of the Revels: The Boy Companies of Shakespeare's Time and Their Plays*. New York: Columbia University Press, 1977.

Shapiro chronicles the history of the amateur and quasi-professional child companies that flourished in London at the end of Elizabeth's reign and the beginning of James's.

The Publication of Shakespeare's Plays

Blayney, Peter. *The First Folio of Shakespeare*. Hanover, Md.: Folger, 1991.

Blayney's accessible account of the printing and later life of the First Folio—an amply illustrated catalogue to a 1991 Folger Shakespeare Library exhibition—analyzes the mechanical production of the First Folio, describing how the Folio was made, by whom and for whom, how much it cost, and its ups and downs (or, rather, downs and ups) since its printing in 1623.

Hinman, Charlton. *The Printing and Proof-Reading of the First Folio of Shakespeare*. 2 vols. Oxford: Clarendon Press, 1963.

In the most arduous study of a single book ever undertaken, Hinman attempts to reconstruct how the Shakespeare First Folio of 1623 was set into type and run off the press, sheet by sheet. He also provides almost all the known variations in reading from copy to copy.

Hinman, Charlton. *The Norton Facsimile: The First Folio of Shakespeare.* New York: W. W. Norton, 1968.

This facsimile presents a photographic reproduction of an "ideal" copy of the First Folio of Shakespeare; Hinman attempts to represent each page in its most fully corrected state.

Key to
Famous Lines and Phrases

Fair is foul, and foul is fair . . . [*Witches*—1.1.12]

So foul and fair a day I have not seen.
[*Macbeth*—1.3.39]

Nothing in his life
Became him like the leaving it. [*Malcolm*—1.4.8–9]

Yet do I fear thy nature;
It is too full o' th' milk of human kindness . . .
[*Lady Macbeth*—1.5.16–17]

Come, you spirits
That tend on mortal thoughts, unsex me here . . .
[*Lady Macbeth*—1.5.47–48]

Look like th' innocent flower,
But be the serpent under 't.
[*Lady Macbeth*—1.5.76–78]

If it were done when 'tis done, then 'twere well
It were done quickly. [*Macbeth*—1.7.1–2]

Is this a dagger which I see before me,
The handle toward my hand? [*Macbeth*—2.1.44–45]

Sleep that knits up the raveled sleave of care . . .
[*Macbeth*—2.2.49]

Will all great Neptune's ocean wash this blood
Clean from my hand? [*Macbeth*—2.2.78–79]

Naught's had, all's spent,
Where our desire is got without content.
                    [*Lady Macbeth*—3.2.6–7]

We have scorched the snake, not killed it.
                    [*Macbeth*—3.2.15]

Duncan is in his grave.
After life's fitful fever he sleeps well.
                    [*Macbeth*—3.2.25–26]

. . . I am cabined, cribbed, confined, bound in
To saucy doubts and fears.   [*Macbeth*—3.4.26–27]

It will have blood, they say; blood will have blood.
                    [*Macbeth*—3.4.151]

Double, double toil and trouble;
Fire burn, and cauldron bubble. [*Witches*—4.1.10–11]

I'll make assurance double sure . . .
                    [*Macbeth*—4.1.94]

Angels are bright still, though the brightest fell.
                    [*Malcolm*—4.3.27]

At one fell swoop?   [*Macduff*—4.3.258]

Out, damned spot, out, I say!   [*Lady Macbeth*—5.1.37]

All the perfumes of Arabia will not sweeten
this little hand.   [*Lady Macbeth*—5.1.53–55]

What's done cannot be undone.
                    [*Lady Macbeth*—5.1.71]

I have lived long enough. My way of life
Is fall'n into the sere, the yellow leaf . . .
[Macbeth—5.3.26–27]

Canst thou not minister to a mind diseased . . . ?
[Macbeth—5.3.50]

I have supped full with horrors.   [<i>Macbeth</i>—5.5.15]

Tomorrow and tomorrow and tomorrow . . .
[Macbeth—5.5.22]

I 'gin to be aweary of the sun . . .   [<i>Macbeth</i>—5.5.55]

Lay on, Macduff,
And damned be him that first cries "Hold! Enough!"
[Macbeth—5.8.38–39]

THE FOLGER SHAKESPEARE LIBRARY

The world's leading center for Shakespeare studies
presents acclaimed editions of Shakespeare's plays.

Hamlet

Julius Caesar

King Lear

Macbeth

A Midsummer Night's Dream

Much Ado About Nothing

Othello

Romeo and Juliet

Shakespeare's Sonnets and Poems

Twelfth Night

For more information on Folger Shakespeare Library Editions, including
Shakespeare Set Free teaching guides, visit www.simonandschuster.com.

SIMON & SCHUSTER
PAPERBACKS
A CBS COMPANY